# A HISTORY OF THE FOOTBALL

TIMOTHY P. BROWN

BROWN HOUSE PUBLISHING

Copyright © 2024 by Timothy P Brown

All rights reserved.

No part of this book may be reproduced in any form or by any electronic or mechanical means, including information storage and retrieval systems, without written permission from the author, except for the use of brief quotations in a book review.

First printing 2024

ISBN: 978-0-9995723-8-2 (eBook)

ISBN: 978-0-9995723-9-9 (Paperback)

Brown House Publishing, Waterford, MI

❦ Created with Vellum

*To Carolyn, with all my love, again*

# CONTENTS

| | |
|---|---|
| *Series Introduction* | vii |
| *Introduction* | ix |
| 1. Shapes and Sizes | 1 |
| 2. Bladders, Lacing, and Valves | 33 |
| 3. Colors and Stripes | 49 |
| 4. Materials and Manufacturing | 65 |
| 5. Game and Practice Footballs | 95 |
| 6. Conclusion | 105 |
| *Notes* | 111 |
| *Bibliography* | 113 |
| *Acknowledgments* | 119 |
| *Also by Timothy P. Brown* | 121 |

# SERIES INTRODUCTION

Since publishing *How Football Became Football* in 2020, I have published over 1,000 articles on my website, *Football Archaeology, and* published a book, *Hut! Hut! Hike!,* in 2022. An unfortunate result of publishing in several formats and across many articles is the resulting lack of integration, making it difficult for readers to understand the game's core elements comprehensively. To correct that issue, this book is the first in the *Football Archaeology Series*, describing how specific components of football originated and evolved.

Much like species in the animal kingdom, football did not evolve along a straight path. It meandered, branched, and detoured with many unproductive twists and turns. And just as mutations in the natural world do not always confer a competitive advantage, players, coaches, media members, and the public have consistently proposed and implemented ideas throughout the game's history that had limited value.

We look back on the ideas that did not pan out as quaint or oddities. Yet, each new idea was an attempt to improve the game or create something new in response to a perceived need. The solution may not have proved valuable, but by highlighting the problem they intended to solve, the oddities tell us as much about the state of the game at the time as the innovations that were accepted or became popular.

In telling the story of how elements of the game evolved, this series covers the rules, equipment, play designs, and other aspects of the game that worked out and, in some cases, those that did not cut the mustard.

# INTRODUCTION

The gridiron football descends from the rugby ball, just as the sport of gridiron football descends from rugby. When gridiron football began, football was rugby, and footballs were rugby balls. There was no difference. Rugby had recently emerged from a mishmash of British folk games that spread from England to its diaspora in the current and former colonies, each forming local governing bodies for their sport. Some locations stayed true to Association Football or Rugby Football Union. Others adapted their game based on regional preferences, resulting in football codes that became Gaelic Football, Australian Rules Football, Canadian Rugby (now Canadian Football), and American Football. As each game evolved, so did the balls used in the games.

American footballers playing under the Eastern college's Intercollegiate Football Association rules used large English rugby balls for the first decade of play before opting for a smaller rugby ball. American football's continued transition into a separate game led to modifying the ball to suit the new game's play and rules. The rugby ball also changed over time, as did the balls used in the other football codes.

As American football transitioned to a separate game, people commonly referred to the sport and ball as rugby and rugby footballs, so it is occasionally unclear in period writing which sport or ball being referenced. That confusion disappeared in the late 1920s when "football" became the nearly universal term for the game and the ball.

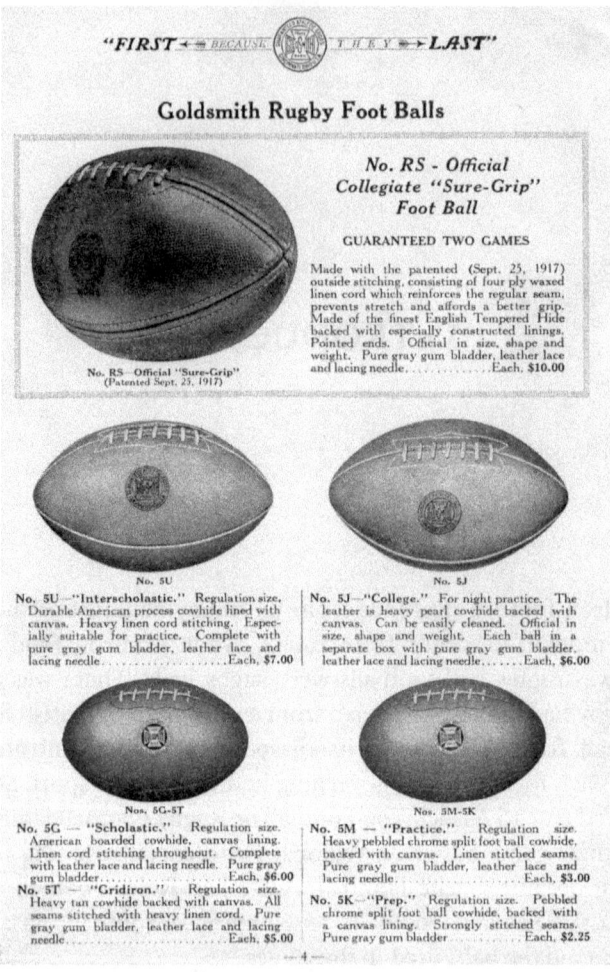

GoldSmith later acquired MacGregor and took its name, so it was among America's top football and sporting goods suppliers in the 1920s. Yet, they still referred to American footballs as rugby footballs in their 1925-1926 catalog. (1925-26 GoldSmith Athletic Equipment, Fall & Winter)

Countless books have covered the history of football or particular periods, teams, and players. However, this book is the first to describe the history of the football itself. The ball has changed its shape, size, construction, inflation levels, and decorations over the years to meet the evolving demands of the game. Yet, despite the many changes to the game since the mid-1930s, the ball has remained essentially unchanged. Other than the emergence of stripes in the 1930s and a minor reduction in the college ball's size in 1982, the football's size and shape are unchanged for ninety years. There have been improvements in the ball's construction, but if someone inserted a fresh ball from the 1930s into a game today, the ball's differences would go unnoticed by most fans and many players.

Almost all the changes to the football occurred before the NFL began exerting its influence over the game, so the story of the football is largely the ball's development in the college game.

This book tells the story of the football in five chapters and starts by examining how the ball's shape and size evolved. The critical changes in the football's history involved the ball's size reduction and reshaping, which occurred in a series of steps lasting nearly fifty years. The ball's size reduction began in the 1800s to make it easier to carry by Americans whose game increasingly shifted away from the Rugby Football Union rules they initially adopted. The influence of the forward pass led to further size reductions so the ball could be thrown more effectively and by more players.

Unlike baseballs or golf balls, footballs belong to the inflated class of sports balls. Chapter 2 tells the story of the football's inflation and how that process changed with new technologies. Since the Dark Ages, English folk games used inflated pig or sheep bladders as balls. Over the centuries, the bladders received leather covers to make them more durable. Later, rubber bladders replaced animal bladders before today's polyurethane bladders took over.

If the ball's size reduction was football's most critical historical change, another fundamental change was its inflation method. That change began in the mid-1920s when manufacturers first produced balls with valves resting flush with the ball's surface. The valves allowed footballs to be inflated without unlacing the leather cover. The laces soon disappeared from the inflated balls used in the world's other major sports, but the football retained its laces because they had become functional for players throwing the forward pass.

Chapter 3 covers cosmetic changes to the football, a more modern phenomenon. Traditionally, footballs were made of tanned leather without adornments because people had the good sense to play football honorably and in daylight. As those conditions shifted, footballs changed colors and acquired stripes to make them more visible when practicing at dusk and playing under the primitive lighting of early night games.

Colors and stripes also helped distinguish the ball from particular team's uniform colors and deliberate attempts to hide the ball.

Chapter 4 examines the materials used to construct footballs over the years and then turns to the manufacturing process, which remains remarkably similar to the methods used at the game's birth. The chapter tells the tale of football production transitioning from an artisan-dominated cottage industry to a tightly controlled assembly line process in a few isolated factories.

Finally, Chapter 5 quickly examines the traditions and rules for the balls used in games and practices and reviews several special-purpose training footballs.

The football history told here is based on evidence from period publications, though it also reflects my interpretation of circumstantial evidence. I surely made mistakes in the storytelling, but if I knew which parts were incorrect, I would have written a different story.

So, *The History of the Football* tells the little-known and underappreciated story of how the football we kick, carry, and pass across the gridiron came to be.

# 1

# SHAPES AND SIZES

Every sport uses particular balls, racquets, goals, and fields or courts. The rules for the field's layout are generally rigid, sometimes allowing for local variations or ground rules. Baseball, for example, enforces a standard height for the pitching mound, the size of the home plate, and the distance and angles between the bases. Yet baseball allows substantial variation in the location and height of the fences surrounding the field, with the distinctive nature of baseball fields being part of the game's charm.

Football rigidly enforces its rules regarding the size of the field and its field markings: the sideline, yard lines, and hash marks, while allowing variation in midfield logos, end zone decorations, and other markings. The ball used in football games today has rigid specifications, but the game had few rules regarding the ball for the game's first half-century. Initially, the game of football used a ball based on custom, with several manufacturers producing balls with similar characteristics. The football's specifications became more detailed only when manufacturing and technological innovations allowed for tighter specifications.

**Football in the United Kingdom**

Today's gridiron football game began in 1876 when students at a handful of Eastern universities formed the Intercollegiate Football Association (IFA) and adopted a slightly modified version of the Rugby Football Union (RFU) rules for the matches played against one another. Neither the RFU nor IFA rules provided specifications for the ball used in their games, but custom called for an oval rather than a round ball. So, understanding the origins of the American football requires a review of how rugby developed and how the rugby ball became customary.

Rugby descends from a stew of folk kicking games played in England dating to the Dark Ages or earlier when religious holidays allowed the serfs to have a few hours of fun. Some games involved kicking leather bottles, tubes, or other objects, but most used an inflated pig or sheep bladder tied off like a balloon. The game rules varied by location, but a common form saw the fellows from one village trying to kick the inflated bladder into the center of a second village, all while the lads from the second village tried kicking it into the center of the first. Tens or hundreds of men might be involved in kicking the bladder until one village penetrated the center of the other and claimed victory.

The games often occurred on Shrove Tuesday, the day before Lent began, and during post-harvest celebrations. Autumn was the traditional time to slaughter pigs, so there were plenty of pig bladders available to inflate and kick. At some point in the history of the kicking games collectively known as football, someone enhanced the ball's durability by inserting the bladder into a leather cover. They inflated and tied the pig's bladder as in the past before closing the leather cover's open seam with thin leather laces. Pigs came in various sizes, as did their plum-shaped bladders, so the leather-covered balls varied in size and were plum-shaped.

Over the centuries, towns and regions developed varying rules for folk kicking games. Likewise, students at Britain's elite schools developed different regulations based on their preferences and the nature and size of the grounds at each school. Some have suggested that schools in urban locations with little green space opted for rules that did not allow tackling, while those in rural areas with more green space allowed the tackling of opponents.[1] Despite the many differences across towns and schools, all were considered a form of football.

In the mid-1800s, graduates of elite schools began arranging recreational football matches, but the inconsistent rules required them to waste time defining the rules for each game, which became bothersome. The changing rules also made developing individual and team skills challenging since practicing and developing skills without knowing which rules would apply in future games was difficult.

These challenges produced a desire to create consistent football rules. After several unsuccessful attempts, a group of clubs formed the Football Association in London in 1863, laying down rules that carry on in the game Americans call soccer. Like other football codes, soccer has evolved from its original rules, including, for example, that the Football Association did not outlaw the use of the hands until 1870.[2]

The Football Association rules did not suit those who preferred a style of play that allowed players to carry the ball. Carrying the ball was a distinctive feature of the game played at the Rugby School in Warwickshire. Since those who preferred the rugby style had the same need as soccer players to formulate consistent rules for their matches, an 1871 meeting led to the formation of the Rugby Football Union. An outcome of the meeting was to name a committee to draft rules for club and international matches, such as the England-Scotland matches, two of which they had already played.

**England's Rugby Ball**

As it happened, William Gilbert opened a cobbler shop in 1823 in Rugby, often supplying shoes and other leather goods to students at The Rugby School. Among those products were balls made of inflated pig bladders with leather covers. The Rugby schoolboys preferred more oval balls that were easier to secure when carried than the round ball, but the balls were so large (slightly bigger than a modern basketball) that the schoolboys fumbled them quite often anyway. Instead, the preference for oval balls primarily results from the difference between the scoring in soccer and rugby. Teams score goals in soccer by kicking the ball between the goal posts and under the crossbar. In contrast, rugby goals occur by kicking the ball between the goal posts and over the crossbar. Since oval balls have more lift than round balls, they fit rugby's scoring rules better and became the norm for rugby moving forward, despite shape and size variations.

The preference for ovoid balls at Rugby appears to have been in place by the 1830s since *Tom Brown's School Days* describes a game that purportedly occurred in 1835 with the ball "pointing toward the School goal."[3]

*1851 Rugby Ball from Crystal Palace Exhibition*

Footballs began their march toward uniformity when Charles Goodyear developed the vulcanization process and a vulcanized rubber ball in 1855. Goodyear's rubber balls achieved popularity, but the more significant impact came through Richard Lindon, another cobbler in Rugby, England. Lindon apprenticed with William Gilbert before opening his own shop, and Lindon also made footballs. In those days, footballs were inflated by mouth using a quill or a clay pipe stem. (William Gilbert's son, Jim, was known for his powerful lungs and ability to inflate rugby balls quickly.) However, inflating balls by mouth was problematic since the bladders were best inflated while still "green," with the result that the person blowing up the bladder sometimes inhaled air from inside the bladder, potentially causing lung infections. Richard Lindon's wife, Rebecca, died from such an infection, leading Lindon to work on developing a vulcanized rubber bladder, which he completed in 1862. Manufacturing rubber bladders rather than using pig bladders allowed for standardizing the bladders' sizes and shapes. In addition, since rubber bladders were more difficult to inflate than pig bladders, Lindon developed a syringe-like inflator or pump to do the inflating.

*Richard Lindon, a cobbler from Rugby, England, standardized the production of association and rugby footballs, formalizing their size and shape. (Richard Lindon. (2024, January 21).*
*In* Wikipedia. *https://en.wikipedia.org/wiki/Richard_Lindon)*

Although Lindon standardized the manufacturing process, he made balls in several shapes: round balls for his soccer-playing customers and oval balls for rugby enthusiasts. Both came in multiple sizes.

FOOTBALLS IN SECTIONS AND COMPLETED.

*Panels and balls of the George G. Bussey & Co. of London. (Harmsworth Magazine, London, 1898; Courtesy of Greg Gugi)*

Lindon's round Punt-about ButtonBalls, so named because the seven-panel ball came together at the ends with large leather buttons, was the template for the Football Association when they standardized the soccer ball at 27 inches in 1872.

Lindon also standardized the shape of the rugby ball based on the size the Rugby School students preferred. Since matches occurred on the part of the school grounds called "Big Side," that ball became known as the Big Side Match Ball. Gilbert joined Lindon in making balls of the same size, and as rugby grew in popularity, the Big Side Match Ball became the ball used in important matches. Still, the Rugby Football Union did not standardize the ball until 1892, when they adopted the following rule:

> The game shall be played with an oval ball of as nearly as possible the following dimensions: length 11 inches to 11 ¼ inches; length in circumference 30 inches to 31 inches; width in circumference 25 ½ inches to 26 inches; weight 12 ounces to 13 ounces; hand-sewn and not less than 8 stitches to the inch.[4]

They amended the ball's weight from 13 ounces to 14 ½ ounces the following year. For comparison, today's football is 21 ¼ to 21 ½ inches at the midsection, while NCAA and NBA basketballs are 29 1/2 to 30 inches in circumference.

**An Evolving Game**

Americans today misperceive 1800s rugby by assuming rugby of the time looked much like it does today. We imagine a game in which the ball pops from the scrum, is picked up and passed to a teammate, who runs wide before passing it to another teammate, who passes it to another, and so on. However, rugby in those days was primarily a kicking game. Players could carry the ball, but most of the action involved players in mauls pushing and kicking the ball forward. Running with the ball was not as manly as overcoming the hacking (aka kicks to the shins) that occurred in close formation. Likewise, soccer was largely a game that saw players dribbling the ball while plowing ahead. There was minimal passing from one teammate to the next.[5]

The form of rugby in which carrying the ball was a primary feature first appeared in America in the 1870s with the "open formation" approach to play. The IFA then reduced the number of players per side from fifteen to eleven, and with fewer players in the mauls and scrums, the ball popped out more often and was picked up and carried. Finally, American football adopted the system of downs and the controlled snap in 1882, leading to quarterbacks picking up the snapped ball on every play and tossing it to a teammate who ran with it, often around the end.

*The 1888 Wake Forest football team with the center still snapping the ball to the quarterback using his foot. (Courtesy of John Gennantonio)*

Rugby later embraced the sweeps that define the sport today, while changes to America's tackling rules led to football in the other direction toward the mass play, run-it-up-the-middle game, forcing us to relearn the sweeping game from our Canadian neighbors in the 1900s.

Whether playing a sweeping or mass game, the style of play placed increased focus on carrying the ball, though kicking remained a central element. Still, the bulbous plum or melon-shaped ball was hard to carry and easily fumbled, so pressure built to reduce the ball's size, occurring in several steps in the U.S. from 1886 to 1934. Likewise, after years of clamoring for a smaller ball for the same reason, the RFU reshaped the rugby ball in 1931, reducing its middle circumference from 25 1/2 to 26 inches to 24 to 25 ½ inches.[6]

**The American Ball and American Rugby Ball**

As in England, Americans played various folk kicking games before the Civil War. Many universities had traditions of mob games played between the freshmen and sophomores under rules unique to each campus. Due to the violence and general mischief, campus or local authorities often banned these games, so students turned to Association football and folk variations that did not allow carrying the ball or tackling that brought opposing players to the ground. The 1869 games between Princeton and Rutgers, widely considered the first college football games, resembled soccer matches, using a round ball with 25 players per side.

Harvard students were an exception for not playing the Association game. They played a game unique to Boston pioneered by the Oneida Club. The Boston game allowed players to carry and run with the ball when pursued by an opponent, with the object of the game being to kick the ball on the fly over the opponent's goal line. (The game did not have goal posts.)

Besides inconsistent game rules before 1876, the type and size of balls varied. Henry Chadwick's *Beadle's Dime Book of Cricket and Foot-Ball*, published in New York in 1866, was among the first to outline rules for football games in America. He laid out 14 football rules and provided other commentary describing a game that combined elements of soccer and rugby. His comments included advice for the ball used in matches:

> With regard to the ball, opinions are divided between the claims of the bladder confined in a leather bag, and a strong india-rubber sphere sold in the shops: we incline to the latter. The ball should not be too large nor too light; as in windy weather too large a ball is a nuisance, and the kick can not be fairly and effectually made.[7]

The India rubber sphere Chadwick mentioned was commonly called the "American ball." The round American ball, made of rubberized canvas, is thought to have originated in Charles Goodyear's workshop. Sold in various sizes, like the Association and rugby balls of the era, it gained widespread use and may have been used in the 1869 Princeton-Rutgers games. Harvard's Boston rules games also may have used the American ball.

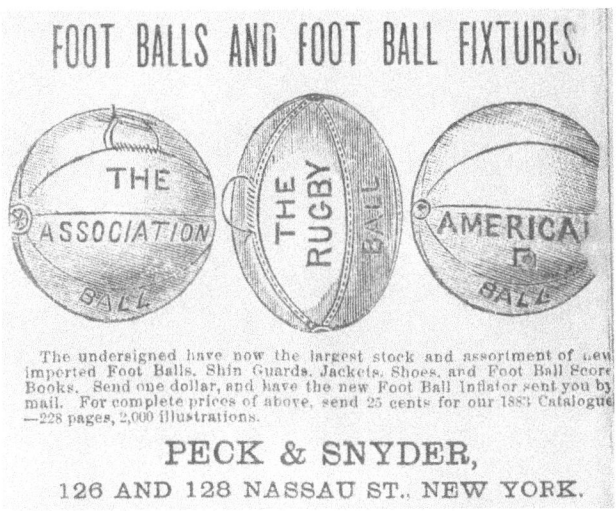

Peck & Snyder ad for three types of footballs. (Camp, Walter (Ed.), Foot-Ball Rules American Intercollegiate Association. Boston- Wright & Ditson. 1883.)

Meanwhile, our latitudinally enhanced Canadian neighbors played rugby under RFU rules since the 1873 Football Association of Canada rules matched the 1873 RFU rules word for word. In May 1874, the rugby-playing students at Montreal's McGill University challenged Harvard to a two-game series in Cambridge, playing one game under Boston rules and rugby rules the next.

The game played under rugby rules convinced Harvard's players that rugby was superior to the Boston game, so the Harvard boys began playing rugby. When Yale and Harvard played in 1875, Harvard's insistence on using rugby rules led Yale to agree to "concessionary" rules combining rugby and Yale's preferred rules. Just as Harvard saw the light when playing McGill under rugby rules, Yale's experience playing Harvard under partial rugby rules convinced them that rugby was superior to their game.

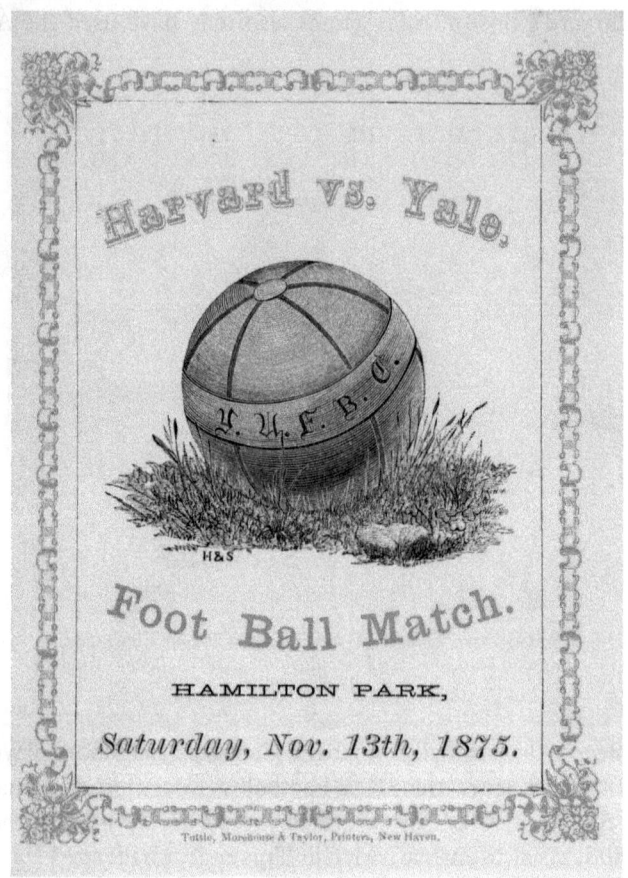

*An American rubber ball appears on the program cover of the 1875 Harvard-Yale concessionary game program. (Wiki)*

During the same timeframe, an All-Canada team of students from McGill and other universities challenged Harvard to a rugby match in Montreal in October 1875. They also played in Cambridge in May 1876 and Montreal in October 1876, with Harvard winning all three games. The Canadians presented Harvard with the game ball after at least one of those matches.

With the leading Eastern colleges playing games under a mix of rules and Harvard insisting on playing only rugby, Princeton invited their counterparts from Harvard, Yale, and Columbia to meet in Springfield, Massachusetts, on November 23, 1876, to formulate a consistent set of rules. By the meeting's end, the group formed the IFA and agreed to game rules virtually identical to the RFU and Foot Ball Association of Canada rules.

Although Yale did not formally join the IFA that year, they followed its rules. The sport of American football descends directly from the rugby rules adopted by the IFA that day. However, fifteen decades of tweaks have produced a substantially different game than the 1876 version of rugby.

One week after the meeting, Yale and Princeton played the first Thanksgiving Day game under the IFA's rugby rules. No one at Princeton owned a rugby ball, so Harvard gave Princeton the game ball presented to Harvard by the All-Canada team. Yale beat Princeton in the match, leading the Tigers to present the ball to the Bulldogs. That ball, which now resides in the Kiphuth Trophy Room at Yale, soon had an engraved silver plaque attached to one side reading:

> *This Ball won by Harvard from the*
> *Montreal F.B. Club ... all Canada.*
> *Presented to Harvard by Princeton*
> *was won by*
> *Yale from Princeton on Thanksgiving Day 1876.*
> *Yale Two Princeton None"*

The ball is the only known example of the type and size of rugby ball used in the first year of American football. A recent measurement shows it is 30 inches in circumference on its long axis and 26 inches at the midsection, making it consistent with the Big Side Match Balls used in English rugby at the time.[8]

*The game ball from the 1876 Yale-Princeton game sitting outside the trophy case. (Yale Athletic Department)*

Rugby players of the era used the Big Side Match Balls by custom since the RFU, Canadian, and IFA rules said nothing about the ball's size, shape, or construction. The lack of rules specifying the ball is notable because rugby and other inflated balls were sold in six sizes from the 1870s through the 1890s, starting at 16 inches in long circumference and increasing in three-inch increments to 30 inches. Multiple manufacturers made the balls, all following a consistent size numbering system for rugby, soccer, and American balls, with the No. 6 having a 30-inch circumference and the No. 5 being 27 inches in circumference. (The numbering system continues today with regulation soccer balls being the No. 5, 27-inch ball, while the regulation rugby ball is the No. 5.)

### GENUINE IMPORTED ENGLISH
# RUGBY FOOT-BALLS.

Best English grain leather, strongly sewed, and warranted to be first-class in every respect. The bladders are made of heavy pure rubber.

| Nos. | 2 | 3 | 4 | 5 | 6 |
|---|---|---|---|---|---|
| Inches in circumference | 19 | 22 | 24 | 27 | 30 |
| Prices | $2.00 | 2.50 | 3.25 | 4.00 | 4.50 |

☞ No. 5 is regulation size.

*Wright & Ditson sold balls ranging from the 19-inch No. 2 to the 30-inch No. 6. (Foot-Ball Rules and Referee's Book. American Intercollegiate Association. Boston: Wright & Ditson. 1889.)*

Some early IFA games may have used the American ball. However, Walter Camp recalled that Yale prepared for the 1876 Harvard-Yale game using a round rubber ball until a shipment of rugby balls arrived a few days before the game, after which they only used rugby balls. So, while they may have used the American ball occasionally, they used rugby balls in IFA games, assuming they were available.

The 1879 Michigan football team pictured with the nearly round ball 30-inch ball of the era. . ("1879 University of Michigan Football Team; BL001001." In the digital collection Bentley Historical Library: Bentley Image Bank. https://quod.lib.umich.edu/b/bhl/x-bl001001/bl001001. University of Michigan Library Digital Collections. Accessed July 21, 2024.)

**Toward A Smaller Ball**

Through the mid-1880s, the size of the ball used in games went unmentioned in the rule books and seldom appeared in the press. One 1876 newspaper reported the IFA agreed to use the No. 5 or 27-inch ball, while another in 1887 that outlined the game's rules mentioned the 30-inch ball.[9] While period images suggest teams used a 30-inch Big Side Match Ball, like the one Yale's trophy case, there is little documentation to confirm the ball's size.

*Shapes and Sizes* 15

*The 1891 Chicago Englewood High School football team, with captain Willie McCornack, holding a melon-shaped football. McCornack later captained and coached Dartmouth. (Personal collection)*

The first specifications for the ball used in American rugby/football came in 1886 when the IFA passed a resolution specifying the use of the English Lillywhite Model J No. 5 model in all matches, notable because the No. 5 was a 27-inch ball.[10] The Lillywhite ball finally received mention in the 1890 rule book in a footnote on the first page, though it does not mention the size:

> Note: The ball used and adopted for the American Intercollegiate Association is the Lillywhite "J" Ball, and is made exclusively for A. G. Spalding & Bros., and to be *genuine must bear their Trade Mark*.[11]

Spalding was the sole agent for Lillywhite balls in the U.S. and manufactured rubberized canvas footballs before they began producing a Spalding-branded leather ball, which the company claims was the first American-made leather rugby ball or football.

## FOOT BALLS.

### THE RUGBY FOOT BALL.
FOR THE RUGBY GAME.

Is oval shape, made of the best India rubber bladder with outside leather case.

**Our Own Make.**

**No. 00.** Spalding's Special Match Ball "Rugby," made of very fine leather. Superior to any football on the market. None genuine unless stamped "*Special Match*" and with our trade-mark. Price, $5.

| | | |
|---|---|---|
| No. 3—22 inch circumference | | $2 50 |
| " 4—24 " " | | 3 25 |
| " 5—27 " " | Regulation size | 4 00 |
| " 6—30 " " | | 4 50 |
| " 7—33 " " | | 5 00 |

### THE ASSOCIATION FOOT BALL.
FOR THE ASSOCIATION GAME.

**Round.**

**No. 0.** Spalding's Special Match "Association" (round), same quality as our No. OO ball. Price, $5.

| | |
|---|---|
| No. 3A—22 inch circumference | $2 50 |
| " 4A—24 " " | 3 25 |
| " 5A—27 " " | 4 00 |
| " 6A—30 " " | 4 50 |
| " 7A—33 " " | 5 00 |

### THE LILLYWHITE REGULATION BALL.

THE LILLYWHITE BALL.

The Regulation English Foot Ball, made by James Lillywhite, Fronde & Co., London, England. We are sole agents for the United States. Regulation Size................................................. $5 00

### RUBBER FOOT BALL BLADDERS.

Made of best India Rubber, a good quality.

| | EACH. | | EACH. |
|---|---|---|---|
| No. 30 for Rugby Ball No. 3,... | $0 80 | 30A Association Bladder,.... | $0 80 |
| " 40 " " " 4,.... | 90 | 40A " " | 90 |
| " 50 " " " 5,.... | 1 00 | 50A " " | 1 00 |
| " 60 " " " 6,.... | 1 10 | 60A " " | 1 10 |
| " 70 " " " 7,.... | 1 20 | 70A " " | 1 20 |

*Spalding ad in Camp, Walter (Ed.), Spalding's Library of Athletic Sports, Foot-Ball Rules, New York, 1890. (Courtesy of John Gennantonio)*

Spalding soon decided they could make more money manufacturing and selling the Spalding-branded ball than being the agents for the imported Lillywhite, leading Julian H. Curtis, a Spalding salesman, to present the benefits of Spalding's American-made Model J football at the IFA's 1892 meeting. The presentation convinced the IFA to adopt the Spalding Model J as its official ball, as noted on the first page of the 1892 rule book. The 1892 rule book also includes a Spalding advertisement showing a letter from the secretary of the IFA indicating that all IFA matches would use the Spalding Model J. The endorsement led many non-IFA teams nationwide to use the Spalding Model J No. 5, or an equivalent 27-inch ball.

The next rule book change related to the football's specifications came in 1896 with the addition of rule 1c:

> The football used shall be of heavy leather, enclosing an inflated bladder. The ball shall have the shape of a prolate spheroid.[12]

Being prolate, the ball was longer along one set of poles than the other, while the football's size remained the subject of a footnote rather than an explicit rule, leading one newspaper reporter of the time to write:

> It is a little remarkable that the size of the ball is not fixed. It is simply required to be "of leather inclosing an inflated rubber bladder.[13]

Despite the rules' lack of clarity, the footnote made the No. 5 or 27-inch rugby ball the official ball, though some teams may have used a No. 6 or No. 4 occasionally.

**Spalding Model J to J5**

The 1892 change to the Spalding Model J No. 5 meant that while football used an American-made ball, it remained a rugby ball in shape, simply smaller than the Big Side Match Ball. Nevertheless, the 27-inch ball was still sizable, and there was apparent pressure to make it slimmer, leading Spalding to release a revised Model J5 in 1903.

Interestingly, Spalding began advertising the Model J as the J5 in 1900, though the ball was unchanged in size, shape, and markings. (The images of the Model J and J5 ball in Spalding's advertisements from 1899 to 1902 are identical.) The 1903 version of the Model J5 had a new shape, markings, and stitching around the laces. In addition, the new Model J5 was 28 inches in circumference along the length and 23 inches in the midsection, making it pointier and more aerodynamic than a rugby ball. In fact, the Spalding J5 was no longer a rugby ball. It had become a football, and as the first of its kind, its new shape would help football evolve in a new direction with the arrival of the forward pass in 1906.

*Note the differences in the shape, marking, and stitching of Spalding's J5 in the 1902 and 1904 advertisements.(1902 and 1904 Spalding Foot Ball Guides)*

The 1903 to 1911 rule books do not mention the Spalding J5 as the official ball and provide no specifications for the ball other than rule 1c with the "oblate spheroid" mention. Oddly, there is no contemporary coverage of the ball changing size in 1903, though it seems an unlikely coincidence that Spalding resized the J5 in the same year it stopped being the official ball. Perhaps some factions wanted to slim the No. 5 ball, and others wanted it to remain the same, but it was not until 1909 that newspaper reports confirmed the ball's middle circumference at 23 inches. It would be three more years before the rule book provided detailed size specifications for the ball, and those only codified the ball already in use.

| American Football Specfications - IFA and NCAA | | | | | |
|---|---|---|---|---|---|
| | Long Axis Circumference | Short Axis Circumference | Length | Weight | Inflation |
| | Inches | Inches | Inches | Ounces | PSI |
| Big Side Match Ball (est.) | 30 to 31 | 25.5 to 26 | 11 to 11.25 | -- | -- |
| 1886 IFA Lillywhite Model J No. 5 | 27 | -- | 11 to 11.25 (est.) | 13 to 14.5 (est.) | -- |
| 1892 AIA Spalding Model J No. 5 | 27 | -- | 11 to 11.25 (est.) | 13 to 14.5 (est.) | -- |
| 1903 Spalding J5 | 28 | 23 | 11 | 14.5 | -- |
| 1912 NCAA | 28 to 28.5 | 22.5 to 23 | -- | 14 to 15 | -- |

*Specifications of the rugby ball or football used in the U.S. through 1912.*

## When Football Came to Pass

When the rule makers legalized the forward pass in 1906, players and coaches struggled to use their newfound freedom. Having never been allowed to throw the ball forward, they struggled to conceptualize plays incorporating the forward pass. Which existing formations favored the forward pass, and what new formations should they employ? Where should eligible receivers go when running downfield, and how should passers time their throw? What should be the responsibilities of offensive linemen who were ineligible to catch passes but could go downfield and block, even while the ball was in the air?

Players and coaches also struggled to identify the best throwing technique. They tried underhand passes, stiff-armed grenade tosses, basketball-like chest passes, and overhand spirals. Some of the challenges of finding the best passing technique resulted from the Spalding J5 and other brand balls being difficult to throw. The football used in 1906 had evolved for use in a game where the ball was kicked and carried, not passed forward. Its rawhide laces barely rose above the ball's surface, the leather was less prominently pebbled, and the ball was substantially fatter than today's. The combination made the ball difficult to grip and throw for anyone who did not have large hands.

Most teams threw the ball occasionally and only in desperation in 1906. However, a few teams used the forward pass effectively with the overhand spiral technique, and none did so as well or as often as St. Louis University (SLU), coached by Eddie Cochems. St. Louis had an end, Bradbury Robinson, the team's punter and primary passer from the punt formation, and John Schneider, who also had large enough hands to throw the overhand spiral. Cochems determined the best approach to passing was the overhand spiral, which he called the "projectile pass" since it traveled fast enough to reach the receivers before the defenders could react. Aided by the forward pass, SLU went 11-0, outscoring their opponents 407 to 11.

Despite their success, Cochems called for football to adopt a slimmer ball to give more players the ability to throw it. Unfortunately, Amos Alonzo Stagg argued against the slimmer ball. Since Stagg was the Midwest's primary connection to the Eastern rule makers, Cochems' call went unheeded, and football did not reduce the ball's size for another 25 years. While Stagg rightly deserved his stature as a football innovator, time proved him wrong on this issue, while Cochems was proven right.

Despite being bigger than today, the 1903 ball was easier to handle than its predecessors, allowing the overhand spiral to become the primary throwing technique as the forward pass gained favor. What might have happened to the forward pass had the ball not become slimmer in 1903? Would it have been less successful in the early years, or would the bigger ball have taken football's style of play in a different direction? And what would have happened to football if the many voices calling for the elimination of the forward pass had won out? Where would the game be today?

**The 1912 Specifications**

It is commonly believed that the football was made slimmer in 1912. It is a story often told, including by me in the past, but there is no contemporary evidence that a change occurred that year. From 1886 through 1902, the rule book specified a Lillywhite or Spalding model as the official ball, so those models defined the regulation size and shape. Then, from 1903 through 1911, the rule book did not identify an official ball. It also did not provide detailed size and shape specifications, so teams could have used a ball of any size or shape. John Heisman reflected on the omission corrected by the 1912 rule change, writing:

> ...so far as the rule was concerned, a team could have brought out a football as big as a barrel had they chosen to do so, and one that weighed a ton, or an ounce, and the other team would have been unable to pull a rule book to back up [their protest], so long as the blooming thing had the right shape.[11]

The 1912 rule did not change the ball's size; it merely specified a ball consistent with the Spalding J5 already on the market and previously considered the official ball. The new rule read:

> The ball shall be made of leather, enclosing a rubber bladder. It shall be tightly inflated and shall have the shape of a prolate spheroid. Circumference, long axis, from 28 inches to 28 1/2 inches; short axis, from 22 1/2 inches to 23 inches; Weight, from 14 ounces to 15 ounces.[14]

Spalding advertisements for the J5 in the 1911 and 1912 Official Foot Ball Guides continued claiming the ball was the "only official college foot ball," with the ball's markings and shape unchanged from those of 1903. Nevertheless, since the 1912 rules for the ball were brand and model-independent, any manufacturer could produce a ball meeting those specifications. As we will see, allowing multiple manufacturers to produce regulation balls opened the door for some manufacturers to skirt the specifications as football's passing game developed.

**Bootleg Balls and 1929 Rule Changes**

Beginning in the mid-1910s, teams increasingly integrated the forward pass into their offenses, and the popularity of the forward pass produced a desire for a slimmer ball. Teams that passed more often than the norm began using slimmer, nonregulation balls in games, which became more prominent in the late 1920s.

The country was then enduring Prohibition, with bootleggers producing or distributing illegal alcohol, so the nonregulation balls became known as bootleg balls. Bootleg footballs hit the news during the 1928 season, and by then, the term described two ways of manipulating the ball. One was the balls that were slimmer than the rules specified. When passing teams hosted a game, they gave the bootleg ball to the referee, hoping neither the referee nor the other team would protest. At the time, schools had the ability to blackball game officials whose rulings they did not like. Since officials who rejected bootleg balls were not likely to officiate that school's games again, they played along to get along.

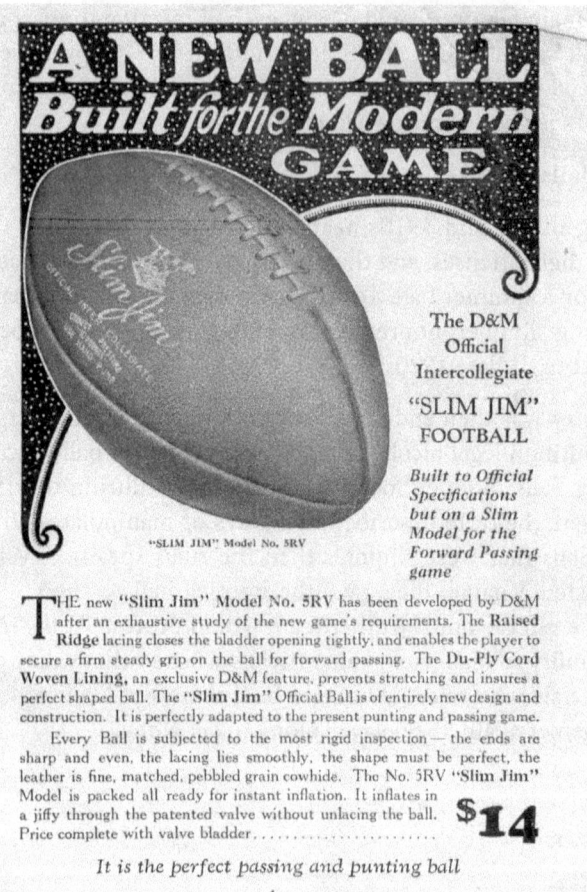

*The manufacturers did not hide the slimmer balls they made. D&M put their Slim Jim on page one of their catalog. (1928 Fall 1929 Winter D&M Athletic Goods Catalog)*

The second type of bootleg ball involved teams overinflating or underinflating the ball. The game's rules did not specify the ball's inflation level, so teams inflated balls based on custom or their preferences. Teams facing a superior punter or kicker might pump the ball with as much air as possible, making it stiff and difficult to kick for distance, and there was nothing an opponent or referee could do about it.

Members of the rules committee monitored the situation during the 1928 season, and following a post-season investigation, they made several rule changes for 1929. First, they reduced the ball's midsection circumference by ½ inch, setting the new standard between 22 and 22 ½ inches.

Second, the mid-1920s witnessed the adoption of valves to inflate footballs, a topic covered thoroughly in the following chapter. Valves allowed the control of the ball's inflation levels, so the rule makers established a standard requiring the inflation of balls to be between 13 and 15 psi.

Third, they instructed referees to measure the game ball before the game and reject out-of-spec balls. Finally, the committee contacted the nation's football manufacturers, warning them not to produce out-of-spec balls. They mentioned that the NCAA could only again approve select brands and models, implying that they would ban manufacturers that did not comply. It seems the manufacturers complied and made only regulation balls, at least for a few years.

An interesting side note is that Canadian football legalized the forward pass in 1929 and also set new specifications for their ball. The Canadian specifications leapfrogged the NCAA's 1929 specifications and adopted a thinner ball that would match the specifications the NCAA would adopt in 1934.

**1934 Size Reduction**

Despite the NCAA instructing manufacturers not to make slimmer footballs after reducing the ball's midsection by ½ inch in 1929, some coaches considered the size reduction insufficient, so they solicited a manufacturer or two to produce smaller than regulation balls. (Ray Morrison, the passing-oriented coach at SMU, and Nokona Leather Goods of Texas are among the likely culprits here.)

After learning of bootleg balls' reappearance, the committee conducted a nationwide survey of coaches, which revealed that most coaches preferred a slimmer ball. Based on that feedback, the 1934 rules reduced the circumference of the ball's midsection from 22 to 22 1/2 inches to 21 ¼ to 21 ½, making it ¾ to 1 inch slimmer than in the past. They did not change other ball specifications in 1934.

Slimming the ball in 1929 and 1934 impacted the game in four ways. First, it allowed more players to grip and throw the ball accurately. Passers no longer had to have large hands to throw the ball well. Second, the ball became pointier, making the bouncing ball more erratic and the path of fumbled balls less predictable and more amusing. Third, the slimmer ball was more challenging to strike when punting, shortening the length of punts, though later changes in technique remedied that situation.

*According to tests performed at St. Louis U, the new ball traveled farther when thrown but not when punted. ('Billikens Given the New 1934 Stream-Lined Football a Test,' St. Louis Star and Times, August 2, 1934.)*

Fourth, and sadly, the pointier football contributed to the demise of the drop kick due to the pointy ball bouncing off the turf less reliably. The drop kick, also challenged by advancements in long snapping and place-kicking techniques, fell into disuse. Of course, drop kickers would have fewer problems on today's artificial turf and manicured grass fields. Still, the speed and precision of specialist long snappers today means there is little need for drop kickers who are less accurate and lack the range of soccer-style kickers.

**The Ball Since 1934**

Despite the rule changes of 1929 and 1934, some teams continued using footballs that strayed from the specifications. Others, like Dutch Meyer at TCU, worked with manufacturers to ensure they received footballs meeting the NCAA's maximum length and minimum circumference, resulting in the skinniest possible ball that remained within the legal tolerances. Other potential abuses led the 1939 rule makers to require referees to check the balls submitted by the home team before each game to confirm they met the NCAA's pressure, weight, and shape specifications. The home team was to provide a pressure gauge, scale, and metal template with a hole cut in a shape that allowed a regulation ball to pass snugly through the hole.

## Shapes and Sizes

**FOOT BALL LACING DEVICE**
No. MF. The most satisfactory lacing device ever invented. Holds ball rigidly..............Each $7.50

**FOOT BALL MEASURING DEVICE**
No. FMD. Made of special light weight durable aluminum composition. Adjustable to minimum and maximum sizes of long axis of foot ball. Complete with steel measuring tape which can be used on both long and short axis..........................Each $7.50

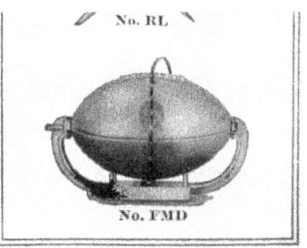

*A football measuring device that preceded the NCAA's 1939 template. (1932 Reach Wright & Ditson Fall & Winter Catalog)*

The shape and size of the football have changed minimally since 1934, though the NCAA made minor changes in 1982. At that point, the long axis circumference was allowed to be 1/4 inch shorter, the midsection circumference fell from 21 ¼ to 21 ½ to 20 ¾ to 21 ¼, or a reduction of ½ to ¼ inches, and the length could be slightly shorter or longer than before.[15]

| | American Football Specfications - IFA and NCAA | | | | |
|---|---|---|---|---|---|
| | Long Axis Circumference | Short Axis Circumference | Length | Weight | Inflation |
| | Inches | Inches | Inches | Ounces | PSI |
| Big Side Match Ball (est.) | 30 to 31 | 25.5 to 26 | 11 to 11.25 | -- | -- |
| 1886 IFA Lillywhite Model J No. 5 | 27 | -- | 11 to 11.25 (est.) | 13 to 14.5 (est.) | -- |
| 1892 AIA Spalding Model J No. 5 | 27 | -- | 11 to 11.25 (est.) | 13 to 14.5 (est.) | -- |
| 1903 Spalding J5 | 28 | 23 | 11 | 14.5 | -- |
| 1912 NCAA | 28 to 28.5 | 22.5 to 23 | -- | 14 to 15 | -- |
| 1929 NCAA | 28 to 28.5 | 22 to 22.5 | 11 to 11.25 | 14 to 15 | 12.5 to 13.5 |
| 1934 NCAA / 1935 NFL | 28 to 28.5 | 21.25 to 21.5 | 11 to 11.25 | 14 to 15 | 12.5 to 13.5 |
| 1982 NCAA | 27.75 to 28.5 | 20.75 to 21.25 | 10.875 to 11.4375 | 14 to 15 | 12.5 to 13.5 |

*Specifications for the rugby ball or football used in the U.S. through 1982.*

## NFL and AFL Balls

Professional football became dominant after the NCAA reduced the ball's size in 1934, so professional football has had virtually no impact on the ball's size and shape other than maintaining the status quo. As we will see in later chapters, the NFL's influence has been on the ball's quality and durability, starting with improving the quality of the leather in the 1950s and the manufacturing quality control measures implemented by Wilson over the decades. Nevertheless, the slight differences in the balls used in the colleges and professional leagues and their effect on passing have been a consistent theme over the years.

Founded as the American Professional Football Association in 1920, the NFL used the NCAA rule book through the 1932 season, so they used a ball meeting NCAA specifications. They adopted Spalding's J5-V as the official ball, which met the NCAA specifications of the time. After the NCAA adopted a slimmer ball in 1934, the NFL did not update its specifications for the 1934 season but did so in 1935 to match the NCAA's 1934 standards.

The NFL ball's specifications of the time read as follows:

> The ball shall be made up of pebble grained leather case (natural tan leather) without corrugation of any kind. The ball shall be inflated with a pressure of not less than 12 ½ pounds and not more than 13 ½ pounds) and shall have the shape of a prolate spheroid – the entire surface to be convex.
>
> The circumference, long axis, shall measure not less than 28 inches, nor more than 28 ½ inches; short axis not less than 21 ¼ inches, nor more than 21 ½ inches; the length of the long axis shall measure not less than 11 inches, nor more than to 11 ¼ inches. The weight of the ball shall be from 14 to 15 ounces.[16]

While wording changes and the added mention of the rubber, now urethane, bladder have occurred over the years, the NFL ball's size, weight, and inflation specifications today are unchanged from those set in 1935.

Changes of another sort came to the NFL in 1941 when New York Giants owner Tim Mara played an instrumental role in the NFL's negotiations with Wilson to replace Spalding as the supplier of the league's balls. For Mara's role in bringing about the change, George Halas recommended naming the ball "The Duke," the nickname of Mara's son, Wellington. The Duke name would appear on NFL balls for several decades.

## Shapes and Sizes

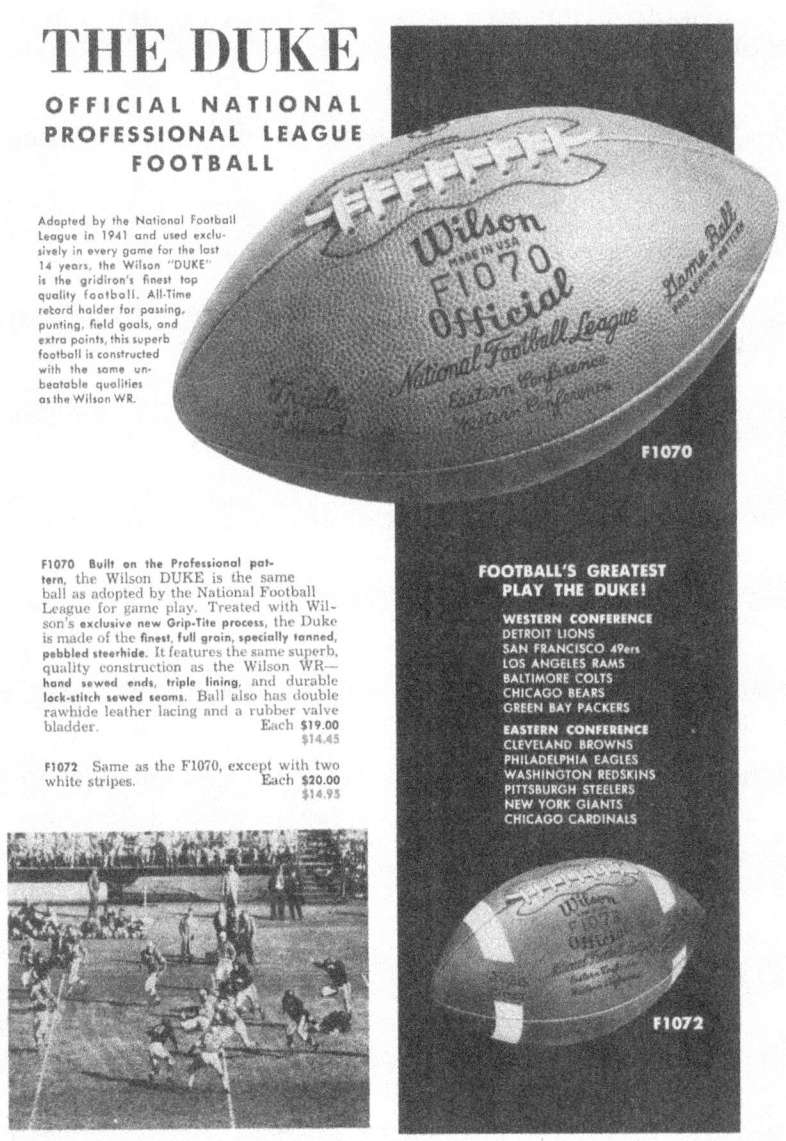

*Wilson was happy to tout its relationship with the NFL in their 1955-56 catalog. (1955-56 Wilson Fall Winter Catalog Trade Price Edition)*

The Spalding J6-V Cushion Control was the American Football League's official ball from its founding in 1960 through the 1965 season. An adaptation of the J5-V, it had an extra layer of cushion beneath the leather and was a quarter-inch thinner and longer. However, the AFL switched to Spalding's J5-V in 1966, a ball matching the NFL's Duke specifications.

The differences between the NFL and AFL balls became a hot topic in the lead-up to Super Bowl I, a game in which the offenses used their league's ball. A newspaper article at the time described the differences in the balls as:

> The balls differ in three areas. 1, The NFL ball (a Wilson) has naturally tanned-in tack, and the AFL ball (a Spalding) is sprayed with a tacky substance after manufacture. 2, The AFL ball is a college-type ball, has a more pointed ogive (the arch) from the laces to the nose of the ball, and the NFL ball is more rounded at the ogive. And 3, the lacing on the NFL ball is 4 1/4 inches long and the lacing on the AFL ball is 4 1/2 inches long.[17]

The ogive, or the ball's shape between the laces and the point, was more rounded on the NFL ball and straighter on the AFL version. To test whether the differences in the balls were noticeable, a sportswriter experimented with Frank Ryan, the Cleveland Browns' Pro Bowl quarterback from 1964 to 1966. The blindfolded Ryan was given an NFL and AFL ball and asked to identify which was which. He could not do so, incorrectly identifying the AFL ball as the NFL ball.

When the NFL and AFL merged in 1970, the NFL continued using a Wilson ball with the same specifications. However, it eliminated the "Duke" name before reinstating it in 2006 following Wellington Mara's death in 2005.

**The CFL Ball**

The path that brought the CFL ball to its current state differed from and overlapped with the American football. The game that is now Canadian football remained more closely tied to rugby for several decades after American football split from the RFU rules. There were regional differences in the Northland, with Western Canada playing a more American-style game than the Easterners.

The Canadian football gained its first specifications in 1906, with dimensions matching the Spalding J5-V. However, their ball was slightly lighter and they allowed either Spalding or Wilson balls that met the specifications. The Canadian ball was made heavier in 1915, so its maximum weight equaled that of the NCAA ball, and another weight change came in 1924.

We noted earlier that the NCAA ball became thinner in 1929 and 1934 due to bootleg balls used by passing teams. When Canadian football adopted the forward pass in 1929, it skipped a step by adopting specifications for the ball that matched those the NCAA would enact in 1934.

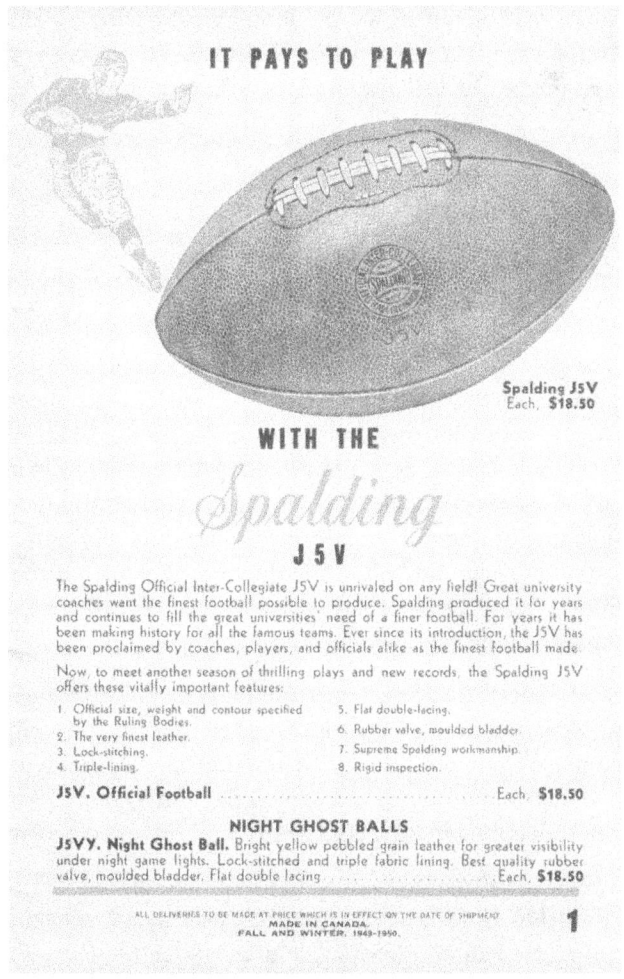

*A Spalding of Canada catalog page touting the tan J5-V and J5VY yellow night ghost ball. (1949-1950 Spalding of Canada Fall and Winter)*

The Spalding J5-V proved popular in Canada over the years, perhaps because Spalding produced the balls sold in Canada at a factory in Brantford, Ontario.

When Canada's western and eastern leagues merged in 1958 to form the CFL, they adopted the Spalding J5-V ball with specifications similar to those of the 1934 NCAA and 1935 NFL balls, except the midsection upper and lower tolerances were 1/8 inch smaller. Another change came in 1986 when the tolerances for the long axis dropped by 1/2 inch and the midsection tolerances dropped by 1/4 inch. These changes made the ball closer to the NCAA ball after its 1982 size reduction.

The CFL used Spalding's J5-V until Spalding closed their Canadian factory. When Spalding proposed supplying the CFL with balls made in South Korea, the CFL switched to Wilson balls made in the U.S.

The CFL's ball changed again in 2018, so its specifications now match the NFL ball's.

**Summary**

The dimensions of the internal organs of domesticated pigs and sheep determined the football's original shape and size. Replacing the animal bladders with rubber bladders allowed the balls' sizes and shapes to be based on the preferences of the various games' players and organizations rather than being biologically determined. The round ball gained favor in Association and Gaelic football, while the oval version was the choice of Rugby Union, Rugby League, Australian Rules Football, Canadian football, and American football.

As American football separated from rugby, the American game's emphasis on carrying rather than kicking led to a reduction in the ball's long circumference from 30 to 27 inches. The continued focus on running the ball led to a second size reduction when the midsection circumference dropped to 23 inches in 1903.

In 1912, rather than specifying a particular brand and model, the NCAA followed the RFU and Canadian football's lead by shifting to specifications detailing the ball's dimensions and weight rather than a brand and model. This change allowed multiple brand and model combinations to qualify as regulation balls.

The legalization of the forward pass led to a new era in football. The pressure to make the ball easier to throw resulted in a two-stage reduction in the ball's size in 1929 and 1934. The NCAA football had another minor size reduction in 1982, while the NFL has used the same size ball since 1935, which matched the dimensions of the NCAA's 1934 ball.

Canadian football remained more rugby-like until it shifted toward American football in the early 1900s. Since then, the game and its football have broadly followed the American path, especially after adopting the forward pass in 1929.

While the coming chapters discuss other changes to the football, the ball's size and shape have changed little since 1935, and the differences across the NCAA, NFL, and CFL have been minimal. While gridiron football uses a ball substantially different than those used in other football codes, the differences between the NCAA, NFL, and CFL have been too subtle to create differences in play across those organizations. While there are differences in play, they are due to factors other than the ball.

# 2

# BLADDERS, LACING, AND VALVES

The previous chapter documented how the football became narrower and smaller, so the discussion now turns to structural changes in the ball. Unlike the largely rule-driven size and shape changes, the structural modifications resulted primarily from manufacturers developing better, more consistent materials to helps balls retained their shape and inflation or to enhance players' ability to grip the ball.

**Inflating and Lacing Early Footballs**

As mentioned, early footballs were inflated pig bladders tied off with string or by tying the bladder like one might tie a balloon. They tied the bladders similarly after encasing them in leather covers. However, by the 1800s, most people inflated balls by inserting a clay pipe stem, quill, or purpose-built nozzle into the bladder's stem and blowing it up the old-fashioned way, using lung power. Inflating the ball by mouth became more challenging when Richard Lindon invented the rubber bladder in 1862, which was stiffer and more difficult to inflate than a pig's bladder. Lindon solved that problem by developing a brass pump modeled after the medical syringes of the day. Inflators that used a rubber bulb, like a bicycle horn, saw use, and sporting goods companies sold both.

Foot-Ball Rules and Referee's Book. American Intercollegiate Association. Boston: Wright & Ditson. 1889.

Wright & Ditson Annueal Illustrated Catalogue, Boston. 1883.

The ball used in the first Princeton-Rutgers game in 1869 deflated several times during the game, and whoever brought the ball forgot to bring their pump and nozzle. When play stopped to inflate the ball, players took turns blowing it up with lung power.

The situation exemplifies how early balls deflated easily and needed regular reinflation. Inflating a football today is simple, assuming you have a needle and pump, but things were not so when Walter Camp and Lorin F. Deland described the process of inflating a football in 1896:

> The ball is a rubber bladder, inclosed within a sack of pigskin; by means of a pump, the bladder is inflated with air up to the limit where it completely fills the pigskin sack, and when the pressure reaches a high point, the mouth of the bladder is securely tied, the pigskin tightly laced, and the

ball is ready for use. It is then practically as a hard as a block of wood, yet of almost no appreciable weight.[1]

The inflation process was subject to variation in the amount of air pumped into the bladder, the air released while tying it off, and the tightness of the knot. One ball might be as tight as a drum, and the next easily indented with a hand squeeze. The variations also affected the speed of deflation, which affected how the ball bounced off the ground on a drop-kick and the distance punters and kickers could boot the ball. At a time when punting and kicking were more critical elements of the game than today, the ball's inflation level impacted the outcome of many games, whether the competitors realized it or not.

The bladders periodically ruptured or leaked, so sporting goods manufacturers and shops sold replacement bladders. By 1900, the bladder stems advanced, so they were less like the stem on a balloon and more like a reinforced nozzle. Manufacturers developed a variety of caps for the nozzles to reduce air leakage.

Rubbers football bladders with a nozzle. (1900 Wright & Ditson catalog)

Despite the advanced nozzles, deflated balls were a regular occurrence. One indication of the frequency of deflation is that manufacturers sold replacement laces and relacing tools, and the manufacturers often included a lacing needle with each ball they sold. These tools made the process as, ahem, seamless as possible.

Two additional tools were the bladder neck inserter and the football lacing device. The tools helped the user stuff the replacement bladder into the leather casing while ensuring the stem or nozzle remained outside the seam while being inflated. On the other hand, the lacing device held the ball in place during the lacing process. The lacing device was handy because the ball had to be fully inflated before lacing it, requiring the lacer to exert significant force to tighten the laces. The device held the ball in place, making the process more efficient and safer. Without the device, a second person often held the ball, subjecting them to injury when the lacing needle slipped or the lace broke during the process..[2]

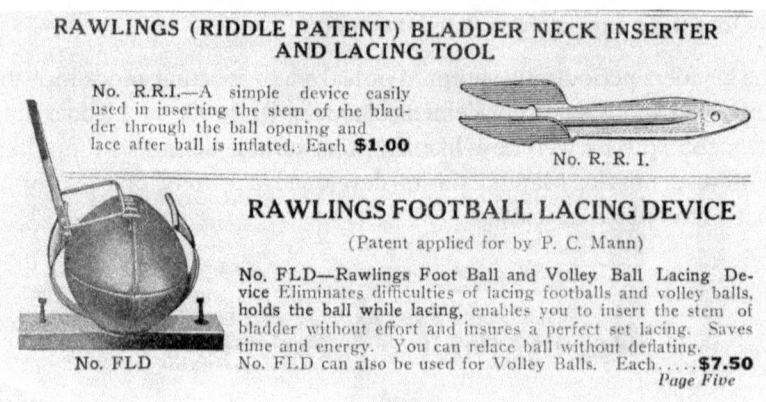

The Bladder Inserter and Lacing Device. (Rawlings Fall 1928 Winter 1929)

The lacing and relacing process required strong but flexible and thin laces, making rawhide the preferred material. A consequence of using thin rawhide laces was that they rose only slightly over the ball's surface. Thin laces were acceptable during football's pre-forward pass days, but passers using the overhand spiral could not generate the torque on the ball as they can with today's laces. That challenge started changing as manufacturers paired rubber bladders with valves in the 1920s.

**Along Came Valves**

Footballs with valves relieved many maintenance headaches, though some in the football community did not immediately embrace them when they arrived in the mid-1920s. The first implementation came by adding Schrader valves to the bladder stem. Schrader valves, which have inflated millions of automobile and bicycle tires since the turn of the last century, were highly reliable and well-understood.

Initially, their value came from reducing air leakage. But balls deflated due to weaknesses in the bladder or other reasons, and a deflated ball had to be unlaced, pumped up, and relaced. By 1923, however, the tinkerers developed a valve with flanges that sat flush with the ball's surface. John Heisman, representing a football manufacturer, presented a valved ball to the 1923 Rules Committee seeking approval of the new valve. Period reports described it as:

> The valve is a rubber disc set into the bladder but all that appears upon the outside of the ball after the inflation has been complete is small half-inch black disc.[3]

The rules committee neither approved nor banned the valves and has not ruled on them since, taking a hands-off approach they have applied to many equipment innovations. The new flush valves saw use in the 1924 season when Notre Dame and perhaps others used a Spalding ball that Knute Rockne received credit for inventing. Rockne soon switched his loyalties to Wilson, where additional innovations occurred.

Most sporting goods companies had high-profile coaches serving on advisory panels and lending their names to the products for marketing purposes. The extent to which certain coaches influenced product development is uncertain, with some coaches focusing on products that addressed their pet peeves.

Rockne lacked the time and tinkering skills to invent the flush valve, more likely offering advice regarding its application. However, there were multiple inventors whose devices were used by the manufacturers as several valve technologies gained popularity. Irl Tubbs, the coach at what is now the University of Wisconsin-Superior, filed a patent on April 4, 1925, and Frank Buechner, a tire shop owner, filed one on July 11, 1925. Either or both could have worked with sporting goods manufacturers before filing their patents, or a mystery inventor might have given us the valved ball. Still, their collective inventions made a critical contribution to various sports.

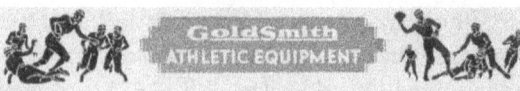

## GoldSmith
### Patented - New and Improved
### Rubber Valve Bladders
(Pat. Nos. 1596320-1520281)

THE Goldsmith All Rubber Valve is the only perfect rubber valve made and is thoroughly covered by patents. It is efficient and automatic in action. This valve contains no metal parts or metal valve cap. Its weight is but the fraction of an ounce. It is the simplest and easiest valve made for quick inflation or deflation.

| | |
|---|---|
| No. GF—Heavy four piece **rubber valve** football bladder | Each, $1.75 |
| No. 5XR—Medium weight four piece **rubber valve** football bladder | Each, $1.50 |
| No. 5XL—Medium weight two piece **rubber valve** football bladder | Each, $1.00 |
| No. GB—Heavy four piece **rubber valve** basketball bladder | Each, $2.00 |
| No. 5XBB—Four piece **rubber valve** medium weight all rubber valve basket ball or soccer ball bladder | Each, $1.50 |
| No. 4XBB—Two piece **rubber valve** basketball and soccer ball bladder | Each, $1.00 |
| No. 4XA—Medium weight two piece **rubber valve** volley ball bladder | Each, $1.00 |
| No. 7XPS—Four piece **rubber valve** regulation weight striking bag bladder | Each, $1.50 |

### Metal Valve Bladders

| | |
|---|---|
| No. GFM—Heavy four piece metal valve football bladder | Each, $1.50 |
| No. 5FM—Two piece metal valve football bladder | Each, 1.00 |
| No. GBM—Heavy four piece metal valve basketball bladder | Each, 1.75 |
| No. 5BM—Two piece metal valve basketball bladder | Each, 1.25 |

### METAL VALVE PARTS

| | | | |
|---|---|---|---|
| No. DC—Dust Cap | Each, $ .07 | No. VK—Valve Key | Each, $ .06 |
| | No. VC—Valve Cap | Each, $ .07 | |

*Illustrations in the top corners of the page show example flush valves. (1931-32 GoldSmith Athletic Equipment, Fall & Winter)*

Sporting goods manufacturers continued making balls with valve stems and those sitting flush with the ball's surface. The GoldSmith advertisement above shows rubber and metal valves sitting flush with the ball's surface, all available for different sports balls. Meanwhile, the Rawlings catalog page below shows an inverted stem bladder that sat inside the bladder, a threaded valve that rose slightly above the bladder's surface, and a stem bladder. Their use of all three suggests that technology was changing quickly as the football world tried to find the best value for the sport.

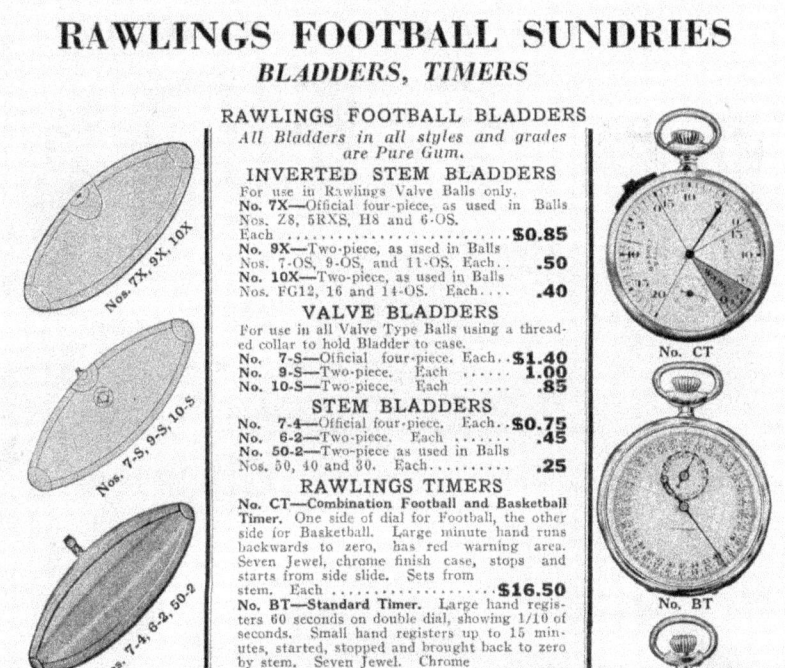

*(1932-1933 Rawlings Fall-Winter Catalog)*

The technology changed because the location and type of valve created dead spots and bulges, while the Schrader valve's weight affected the ball's flight, so the manufacturers tried to work through issues affecting the ball's performance by

While the manufacturers addressed those problems in time, valved balls proved more reliable and far easier to maintain than those without. Initially, valved balls were used for higher-end balls for the college and high school markets, with stemmed balls targeted at the recreational market. By the early 1930s, only budget balls and those used for children's play still had stems.

Using valves created the need for teams to stock gauges, wrenches, and replacement parts because even the best valves failed from time to time. Top-of-the-line gauges showed their results on a dial, while others used the less reliable but cheaper sliding bar. In addition, many valves had caps to keep dirt and dust from plugging them.

40 A HISTORY OF THE FOOTBALL

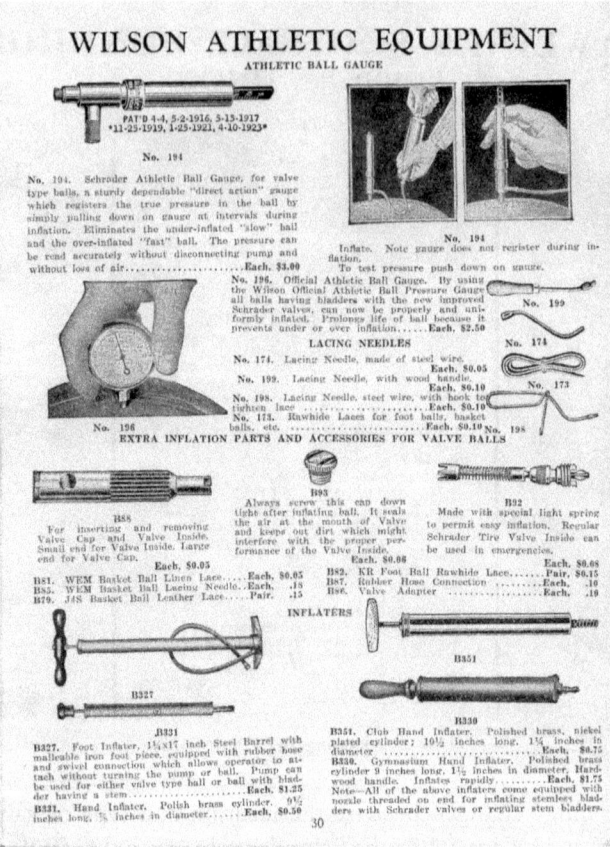

Football equipment managers needed more tools and replacement parts to keep their footballs in playing shape. (1928-1929 Wilson Catalog Fall and Winter)

Most important, flush valves allowed balls to be reinflated without needing to unlace and relace them. The valves also allowed balls to maintain consistent pressure, opening the door to introducing a new specification for game balls: a target inflation level.

## Football Under Pressure

Chapter 1 mentioned the late 1920s and early 1930s bootleg footballs, focusing on slimmer balls that gained popularity among passing-oriented teams. Another form of bootleg balls dealt with their inflation levels, which might be called Inflategate today. Instead of balls structurally different from the norm, coaches who did not have strong punters or kickers sometimes inflated the game balls to very high levels to make them challenging to punt or kick for distance. Technically, the balls were not overinflated since football did not have an inflation standard. They were just inflated to higher levels than the norm, whatever that was. And just as Heisman had commented in 1912 that the ball could have been as big as a barrel before the rules specified the ball's size, the lack of an inflation standard meant balls could be as soft as a pillow, hard as a rock, or just right.

To deal with the inflation issue, the NCAA's rule makers of 1929 added football's first inflation requirements, requiring the ball to be:

> ... inflated with a pressure of not less than 13 pounds nor more than 15 pounds and shall have the shape of a prolate spheroid - the entire surface to be convex.[4]

The new rule required game officials to check inflation pre-game, forcing the use of valved balls in games since the gauges that measured inflation levels worked only with valved balls.

## Lacing Them Up

By the time valved balls came along, the forward pass had been legal for over 15 years, and the overhand spiral had become the primary means of throwing the ball. The presence of laces assisted in throwing the overhand spiral, so the football's laces served a function beyond temporarily sealing the ball. Not so with basketballs, soccer balls, volleyballs, and rugby balls, so the manufacturers immediately began eliminating the laces from those balls. Like Rockne, Wisconsin's basketball coach, Walter Meanwell, teamed with Spalding in 1925 to "invent" a valved basketball without external lacing, called the hidden lace basketball. For a time, the manufacturers continued selling laced balls for sports other than football due to customer preferences and the lower costs of those balls. Still, external laces largely disappeared from the balls used in other sports by the late 1930s.

Football laces followed a different path. Thin, flexible rawhide had been the preferred lace since cobblers first encased pig bladders, but with the ball no longer needing to be unlaced and relaced to be reinflated, the functional requirements of the laces changed. Pre-valve footballs typically had six leather cross laces barely rising above the ball's surface, but valved balls allowed manufacturers to optimize the lacing for passers rather than equipment managers. The change in requirements led to changes in the number of stitches, their pattern, and the composition of the laces.

The 1918 Reach catalog featured their best ball, which had six laces. (1918 Reach Fall & Winter Catalog)

The first change came in the number of laces. Pre-internal valve footballs generally had six cross laces, but valved footballs soon had seven to ten cross laces on top-of-the-line balls, while less expensive balls had fewer cross laces. Regardless of their brand or cost, almost all footballs converted to eight cross laces after WWII, but the number varied until the NCAA required footballs to have eight cross laces in 1975. Most footballs today have eight cross laces, though high school footballs can have up to 12 today.

Another critical change in football lacing came with double lacing, which premiered on Wilson's Knute Rockne ball in 1929. Until then, the external lacing only ran perpendicular to the seams.

The Rockne Double Laced ball had two long lengths of external lacing running parallel to the seam, under and perpendicular to the cross laces. The design raised the height of the laces to ensure "a firmer grip when passing."[5]

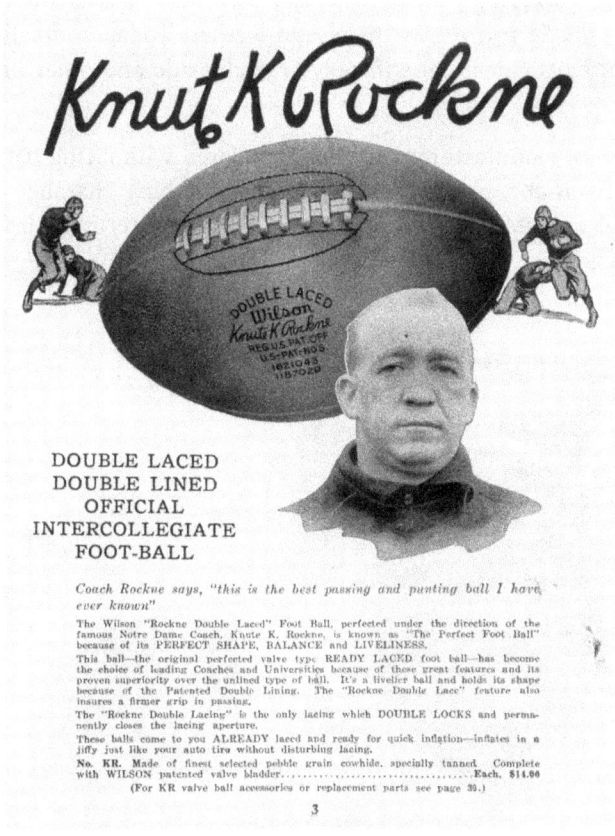

(1928-1929 Wilson Catalog Fall and Winter)

The double lace pattern results from the cross laces on the ball's exterior, tying the punched holes opposite one another on either side of the seam. Another stitch runs inside the cover, angled between sets of holes. As in the past, lacers still used a lacing tool like a large crochet hook to pull the lace through the holes and tighten the stitches.

Double lacing was more complex but it raised the laces further above the ball's surface to aid passers throwing the ball. In addition, since valves reduced how often balls were unlaced and replaced, the manufacturers began using stiffer and thicker lacing, which raised the laces further above the ball's surface and provided more resistance for passers. The combination made the ball easier to throw by maximizing the torque generated as the ball left the passer's fingertips.

Leather laces gave way to woven linen and proprietary formulations combining leather and other materials. Rawlings balls of the late 1950s used laces made from "Daw-hide" and leather. Today, football laces for regulation balls consist of stiff polyvinyl chloride and other proprietary materials.

In the 1930s, manufacturers also experimented with lacing patterns that differed from the parallel, evenly-spaced stitching that had been the norm. Wilson offered traditional stitching and patterns with five Xs or cross stitches.

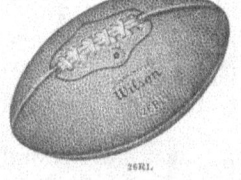

*Wilson offered a ball with eight cross laces and three in an unconventional pattern. (1930-1931 Wilson Fall and Winter catalog)*

Rawlings introduced the Zuppke ball, named after Illinois coach Robert Zuppke, which had cross stitches between the fifth and sixth laces. The cross stitches were supposed to maintain a tight seam so the ball did not lose its shape.

*The Zuppke ball had on cross stitch in the center of the laces. (1932-1933 Rawlings Fall and Winter Sports)*

While Rawlings believed a cross stitch between the fifth and sixth laces produced a ball that maintained its shape, Reach sold its two-seam Air-Flite ball with ten cross stitches and a gap between the fifth and sixth seams during the 1934 season.

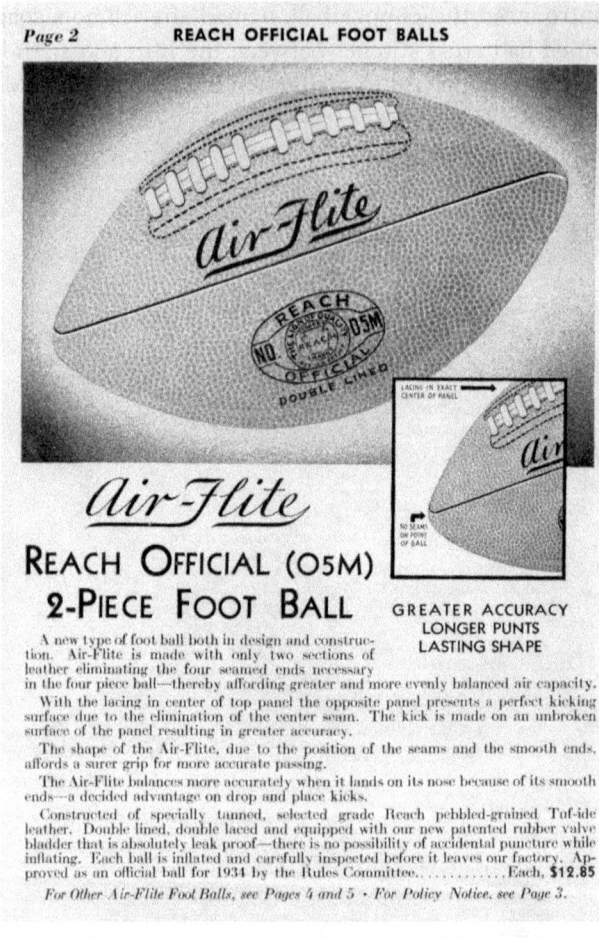

Reach's ten cross-lace ball with a middle gap. We will discuss this ball further in Chapter 4. (1934 Fall 1935 Winter Reach Wright & Ditson Catalog)

The cross-stitching patterns lasted only a few years, so the stitching either had little impact or the manufacturers found other methods to maintain the ball's shape.

**Summary**

Despite most people paying little attention to changes in the guts of footballs, the march of materials science has resulted in footballs composed of materials better suited to their function. The primary purpose of a football's bladder is to inflate the ball, keeping it stiff by limiting air leakage. Manufacturers switched from animal bladders to natural rubber in the

1800s, and then to synthetic butyl rubber bladders in the 1950s, and polyurethane bladders in the late 1980s. These bladders are now so effective at retaining air that few recognize how easily balls deflated in the past. As shown in this chapter, manufacturers of the early 1920s guaranteed their balls to remain inflated and retain their shape for only two games, a standard that would be wholly unacceptable today.

Players, coaches, and equipment managers of the era accepted that unlacing and relacing footballs were part of preparing for practices and games. The arrival of internal valves largely eliminated that need. With the footballs' increased reliability, manufacturers modified the lacing patterns and materials to better suit the passing game. Unlike many other sports, gridiron footballs retained their laces because they took on a second function different from their original purpose, which had become largely irrelevant.

We have it comparatively easy today. The only footballs most of us have ever inflated are those that sat on an office or garage shelf for years. The footballs in the active rotation of teams or those we toss around in the backyard typically wear out due to losing their pebbling rather than losing their air.

Likewise, an increasingly smaller number of us have practiced or played in games under lighting poor enough to make it difficult to see an unstriped tan ball. Yet, that experience was familiar to our football ancestors and is the subject of the next chapter.

# 3
# COLORS AND STRIPES

In addition to changes to the football's size, shape, bladders, and lacing, the ball has undergone cosmetic changes due to five historical influences, most of which had a functional basis.

The first factor to influence the appearance of football was durability. Footballs began as inflated animal bladders made more durable when covered with leather. While we will discuss at least one serious candidate to replace leather as the ball covering, leather remains today's preferred cover.

The second set of cosmetic changes resulted from a desire for improved visibility. Teams painted footballs white, yellow, or red to make them easier to see on poorly lit practice fields and later for games in dimly lit stadiums.

The third factor influencing the football's appearance was camouflage, or, more correctly, the opposite of camouflage. At times, concerns were raised about teams whose uniform coloring made it more difficult for defenders to identify which offensive player had the ball. Whether it was tan pants, helmets, and patches on the jerseys or white uniforms that concealed snazzy white footballs, the camouflage concern helped drive the addition of striping on footballs.

The fourth driver of the ball's appearance has been handedness. Handedness concerns led to eliminating or shifting the ball's stripes to ensure that passers' thumbs did not rest on paint, which those insufferable quarterbacks claimed made the ball more slippery.

The fifth influence is branding. While more amorphous than the first four factors, eliminating or retaining the stripes on the balls used at different levels has served as a means of branding and distinguishing college, CFL, and NFL balls.

**Durability**

As covered in previous chapters, the ancestors of our gridiron football emerged from games played when most residents of the British Isles were peasants. Those peasants occasionally found an animal bladder worth blowing up, leading them to spend an afternoon joyously kicking it around. After several centuries, an intelligent peasant recognized that covering the animal bladder with leather made the ball last longer. Longer-lasting balls were convenient and more posh, especially the well-made balls sold to schoolboys by local cobblers.

The ball was tan or brown because that was the color leather took on during the tanning process, and there was no particular reason to color the ball differently.

**Visibility**

The emergence of football in colors other than tan or brown resulted from the desire to practice and play under artificial light. Thomas Edison filed his first patent for electric light bulbs in October 1878, two years after the IFA met to define football's first rules. The initial games played under electric lights occurred indoors in orchestra and exhibition halls, while the first known outdoor game played under the lights came in 1892 when Mansfield State Normal met Wyoming Seminary. The combination of poor lighting and fog led them to stop the game at halftime. Similar lighted outdoor games occurred here and there before lighting technology improved to allow semi-regular night games in the 1920s.

While there were attempts to play at night, games that ended in darkness were more common because games traditionally started at 2:00 P.M. or 2:30 P.M. The start times allowed fans to do chores or work on Saturday morning while giving visiting teams time to travel to the game location by train. Most games finished within two hours, so artificial lighting was necessary only when the match started late or ran longer than usual.

Things got worse after the introduction of Daylight Saving Time in 1918. After several years of late-season games ending in the poor light of dusk, a 1922 rule allowed referees to confer with the team captains at halftime to shorten the second half if needed. Some schools combatted the problem by starting their games an hour or two earlier, a few lit their fields, and others painted their footballs white, yellow, or red to increase their visibility.

The earliest reference to footballs that are not tan or brown came in 1901 when late classes forced Amos Alonzo Stagg's University of Chicago team to practice under the lights. Stagg had his team use a white football when practicing under their primitive lighting system.

White footballs became more prominent in the 1920s as teams began playing semi-regular night games due to advances in lighting technology and the stadium-building boom. Teams painted the balls until the manufacturers began offering white or yellow versions of their higher-priced balls by the early 1930s. Early on, the catalogs did not show examples of lighter-skinned or "ghost" balls but later included images of white balls among their offerings.

No. 5RVW. "GHOST" FOOTBALL. An all white football for use in late afternoon practice during the end of the season when it gets dark early. Also an ideal football for use in night games under flood lights. Conforms in every detail to the Rules Committee specifications. Made of chrome tanned white cowhide. Double criss X cross fabric lining. Double "hold fast" lacing, patented valve type bladder of pure gum rubber..........Price $14.00

[ 1 ]

*Ghost balls were for sale but not pictured in D&M's 1930 catalog. (1930-1931 D&M Athletic Goods Fall and Winter Catalog)*

## Camouflage

Besides painting the tan ball white, yellow, or red, a few teams added stripes to help players and fans better see the ball at night. Besides aiding visibility, colors and stripes mitigated the camouflage effect of teams wearing leather helmets and friction strips or patches on their jerseys in colors similar to the ball. In addition, the increasing use of white jerseys in the late 1920s and 1930s presented problems when they used white balls for night games.

Among the first high-profile cases of camouflaging was the 1926 Illinois-Penn game. A controversy arose from a report that Illinois coach Bob Zuppke was upset that Penn wore tan-colored patches on their chests and sleeves as part of their hidden ball offense. Supposedly, he informed Penn's coach, Lou Young, that they would play the game with a white ball unless Penn removed the offending patches. The parties subsequently claimed the reported controversy was fanciful, but true or not, it raised the profile of the potential trickery.

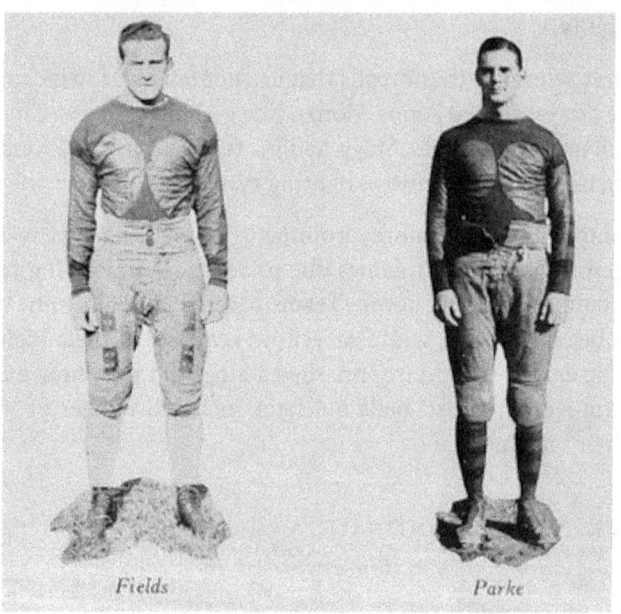

Penn players wore friction strip patches in the same color as the ball, which many considered deceptive. (*1927 Pennsylvania Record yearbook*)

Teams facing a white-jerseyed opponent at night sometimes refused to play with an all-white ball lest their players have difficulty spotting the white ball in the arms of the white-jerseyed opponents. Cincinnati planned to use a yellow ball when playing white-jerseyed Kentucky Wesleyan in 1929 after falling victim to the white jersey-white ball trick in their 1928 game. The first Big Ten night game, Purdue's 1935 visit to Northwestern, employed a white ball with black stripes due to the Wildcats wearing white jerseys home and away. Another controversy that year arose before the BYU-Northern Colorado night game. Northern Colorado objected to using a white ball due to BYU's white jerseys, while Northern Colorado's brown pants made BYU object to using a brown ball. Ultimately, the coaches agreed to paint white stripes on a brown ball, the first known instance of that design's use in a game.

Following reports that certain running backs tossed their tan helmets to the ground during play to simulate fumbling, the NCAA's 1930 Rules Committee required that helmets have at least two cross stripes of a markedly contrasting color at least two inches in width while jerseys similar in color to the ball had to be broken by stripes or numbers in distinct colors.

The NCAA Rules Committee formally approved white footballs in 1930 and mandated black stripes on either end in 1941. The 1940 GoldSmith catalog offered two versions of the white ball. One had thin black stripes painted along the length of the ball's seams, a design that was not popular. GoldSmith also offered a ball with the one-inch stripes we all know and love, though the stripes were shifted toward the ball's center, overlapping the laces.

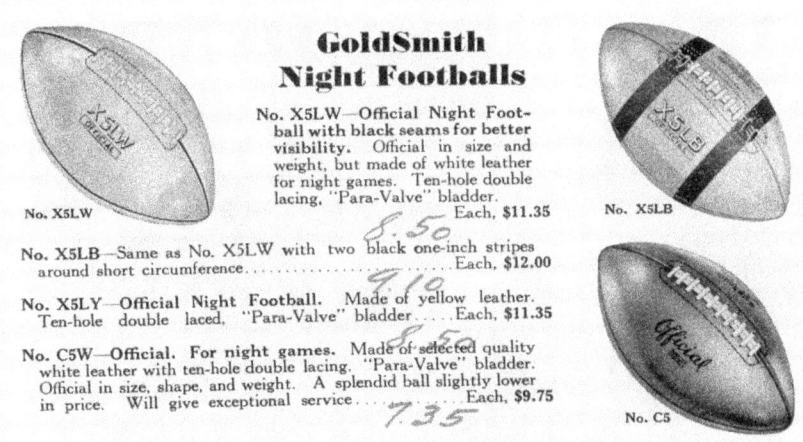

GoldSmith's night footballs saw the light in their 1940 catalog. (1940 GoldSmith Preferred Sports Equipment Fall & Winter)

Various high school organizations mandated white and yellow footballs with stripes for night games in the 1940s. They remained in use until the 1950s, when stadium lighting improved, and tan balls with white stripes became the standard.

## Striping

Everyone watching football today knows where the stripes belong on the ball. Few of us remember when the single stripe at each end of the ball was in a different location or when there was more than one stripe at each end. However, those days existed because it was not immediately apparent where to locate the stripes or how many there should be.

Besides the single stripes that overlapped the laces in the previous image, some footballs had double stripes. The *1949 MacGregor GoldSmith Fall and Winter* catalog offered several Official Night Football versions of their M5G. Teams could order white or yellow balls with one or two black stripes. The single stripe and inner stripes were closer to the ball's center than today, so they overlapped the laces. The catalog also offered a tan leather football with two one-inch white stripes on either end.

*McGregor offered single, double, and no-stripe versions of the football.*
*(1949 MacGregor GoldSmith Fall and Winter catalog)*

After several years of manufacturers offering balls with different stripes, the National Federation of State High School Athletic Associations (NFHS) recommended that teams use balls with one stripe on each end in 1952. Their recommendation stemmed from the fact that multi-striped balls created an optical illusion as they flew toward receivers.

*Double-striped tan ball in use during a 1952 night game. (1953 Occidental College La Encina yearbook)*

In 1953, the NFHS required tan balls with white one-inch stripes 3 to 3 1/4 inches from each end, though schools could use the more expensive white or yellow footballs for night games if approved by their conference or both coaches. The football's stripes remain in the same location on NCAA, NFHS, and CFL balls today,

Various teams used tan balls with white stripes in the 1940s and 1950s, though most night games used white balls or white balls with black stripes. The NFL stopped using white balls for night games in 1956, substituting a tan ball with white stripes. Notably, the plain tan ball remained the mainstay of college day games until 1975, when the NCAA required tan balls with white stripes for all games.

*A tan ball with white stripes shifted toward near the middle makes an appearance in a late 1940s game. (1950 Florida State Tally-Ho yearbook, courtesy of the Florida State University Libraries, Special Collections and Archives)*

The variation in football colors and striping patterns provides an example of football's history of experimenting with different solutions before settling on a standard. So, why did colored footballs, double stripes, and stripes overlapping the laces disappear? The primary reason for the disappearance of double striping was the visual effect of the double stripes as they spiraled toward receivers. And the double-striped ball's days were numbered once the NFHS mandated the single-striped ball.

The balls' coloring and the stripes' location were another matter. Although some white balls were tanned white, the manufacturers painted most white and yellow balls. Likewise, they painted the stripes on the ball's surface, which affected the passer's grip. By the 1950s, quarterbacks were operating out of one T formation or another had become the game's primary passers. Finicky quarterbacks like Otto Graham did not like fully painted balls or stripes shifted toward the ball's center, which forced them to place a finger or two atop painted laces, so painted balls disappeared, as did stripes overlapping the laces.

**Signature Striping**

Another once-common striping variation included gaps in the stripes on one of the ball's top panels to allow for commissioner signatures and branding. Like other balls in the 1950s and 1960s, the striped NFL ball had these gaps.

The Wilson F1072 ball was the official NFL ball, with gaps in the stripes on one top panel. (1956-57 Wilson Fall Winter Catalog Trade Price Edition)

Returning to the finicky quarterback theme, the same concerns about paint on the ball led to football's brief dalliance with right and left-handed footballs and the striping pattern used on college balls today, at least those used by American colleges.

**Right and Left-Handed Footballs**

We seldom think of balls as right—or left-handed, but there was a period when NFL footballs were both right—and left-handed. The handedness issue arose because the stripes were located where quarterbacks rested their thumbs when gripping the ball.

Otto Graham complained about the thumb-on-paint problem by 1950, but no one did anything about it until the San Francisco 49ers' John Brodie took action. From 1956 through 1975, the NFL used unstriped tan balls for day games and tan balls with white stripes for night games. The story goes that Brodie disliked having his thumb rest on the stripes, so he scraped the paint off the 49ers' night game footballs in the spots where his thumb rested.

Brodie's actions led the NFL to change its paint pattern to accommodate right-handed quarterbacks. The new ball had stripes on both top panels and the sides of the bottom panels opposite where the quarterback's thumbs rested, so each bottom panel had one stripe. The NFL game-used ball from 1970 shown below has signature striping on one of the top panels and right-handed striping on the bottom panels.

*The signature striped top panel of an NFL ball from 1970 with Pete Rozelle's signature. (Heritage Auctions / HA.com)*

*One of the right-handed bottom panels on the same NFL ball. (Heritage Auctions / HA.com)*

While the NFL's striping pattern solved the problem for right-handed quarterbacks, it did not help southpaws, which became a problem when Ken Stabler and Bobby Douglas entered the league in 1968 and 1969. Both were left-handed and while the stripes did not concern Bobby

Douglas, Stabler followed John Brodie's lead by scraping the paint off the ball where his left thumb rested. (Another version indicates the Raiders' equipment manager did the scraping.) The situation led the Raiders' general manager, Al Davis, to appeal for balls suited to left-handed quarterbacks, which the NFL introduced during the 1970 exhibition season. The striping on the bottom panels of left-handed balls was opposite the right-handed balls, and they marked left-handed balls with an "L" and righthanded balls with an "R." The marking helped game officials ensure they had right-handed balls on the field for righties and left-handed balls for lefties. After six years of this tomfoolery, the NFL solved the problem in 1976 by eliminating the striped ball, and they have been stripeless ever since.

Meanwhile, the NCAA approved tan balls with white stripes in 1965. Due to the same issue with quarterbacks and their thumbs, the NCAA implemented a one-year rule in 1974 that allowed teams to use balls with stripes on two, three, or four panels. The one-year rule allowed schools to use their inventory of three and four-panel balls, knowing that balls striped only on the top panels would be legal in 1975. Since the stripes appeared only on the top panels (those next to the laces), the striping did not interfere with the thumb placement of righties or lefties.

Meanwhile, Canadian professional football sometimes used white balls with black stripes for night games. By the early 1960s, they had switched to tan balls with white stripes for CFL night games, and the CFL adopted the tan ball with white stripes for all games in 1964 (or thereabouts).

Then and now, the Canadian football's stripes encircle the ball's four panels. That means American quarterbacks, who comprise the majority of CFL quarterbacks, somehow throw tight spirals in Canada despite the painted stripes on the bottom half of the ball. While Wilson sews composite pebble grain stripes on their GST balls, and the CFL used sewn-on stripes in 2006, they returned to painted stripes the next year and continue using them today.

*Wilson CFL Football*

**The Visually Enhanced Ball**

Charlie Finley, who owned baseball's Oakland Athletics from 1960 to 1980, enjoyed challenging the norm, particularly concerning uniform and equipment aesthetics. He was the first to have his baseball team take the field wearing white spikes rather than black, and he promoted the use of orange baseballs, which did not gain acceptance because hitters could not pick up the ball's spin.

Finley also owned the NHL's Oakland Seals and the ABA's Memphis Tams, but his only foray into owning a professional football team was a proposed league combining U.S.-based teams and the CFL. He was to own the league's Chicago franchise, but that version of U.S. teams in the CFL did not materialize.

Still, the football burr remained under Finley's saddle, leading him to devise two changes to the football, which he marketed through Wilson and Rawlings. Finley filed a patent application for the Visually Enhanced Football in May 1989 and the Grip Enhanced Football (aka the Double Grip) in September 1989. (We cover the Grip Enhanced Ball in the next chapter.)

Rather than a single stripe at either end of the ball, Ol' Charlie applied eight half-inch longitudinal stripes running along the ball's seams. He reasoned that his pattern helped everyone better see the ball at night, particularly in high school stadiums with less effective lighting. Thinking the striping pattern also made sense for daylight games, they produced a night version with fluorescent yellow stripes and a day version with white stripes.

*The Visually Enhanced Football on either side of a traditionally-striped college ball. ('New Footballs Add Color To Sport,' Indianapolis News, November 2, 1989)*

The Visually Enhanced Ball stripes sat on either side of the ball's seams, reaching nearly to the tips and stopping about an inch short of the laces. The Visually Enhanced Ball supposedly saw its first use in two different Indiana and one Florida high school games. (The duplicate claim likely was due to Finley promoting each game as the ball's premiere.) High schools in eight or nine states used the ball in 1989, providing mixed feedback. Fans thought the ball was easier to track when spiraling through the air, and a game official noted the longitudinal stripes made it easier to track the ball in the air as it tumbled end-over-end on field goal attempts. However, some receivers thought the ball was more difficult to catch because it was harder to distinguish its outline than balls with transverse stripes.

Not to be deterred, Finley convinced the powers that be to use the ball in the 1989 Blue-Gray Game and the 1990 Hula Bowl. He also pitched his ball to a cooperating rules committee for the high schools and NCAA, which resulted in the NFHS allowing its use, assuming both teams agreed.

Despite the NFHS approving its use, the Visually Enhanced Ball did not gain acceptance, disappearing from the scene as quickly as it had arrived. Teams did not see sufficient benefits from the alternate striping pattern to justify stocking them. Also, a legal issue did not help the situation, which we will cover in the next chapter.

## Branding

White stripes increased the ball's visibility and countered attempts to camouflage the ball, but those reasons no longer or seldom apply to today's game. No one wears the leather patches, pads, or earth-tone canvas pants that were nearly universal through the 1920s. Likewise, today's stadium lighting conditions mean white stripes are no longer needed.

Instead, white stripes and their absence serve branding purposes more than on-the-field functionality. The NCAA's public pronouncements for adopting the white-striped ball in 1975 were the improved visibility and the desire to use the same ball for day and night games. That rationale made sense when the NFHS adopted the white-striped ball in 1953, but the CFL did so around 1964 and the NCAA in 1975. By then, stripes were seldom necessary for night games and only at poorly lit facilities, and no one needed them for day games. Instead, the stripes result in balls visibly distinct from those used by the NFL.

Using a ball with a distinctive look fits the NCAA's longstanding antipathy toward the NFL. From the early blackballing of game officials who worked NFL games to forbidding the mention of the NFL during NCAA television broadcasts in the 1960s, distinguishing the games has been essential to those at NCAA headquarters.

The same attitude was on display in the mid-1980s. Despite minor differences in the specifications of NFL and NCAA balls, they were physically interchangeable, so some schools used NFL balls painted with white stripes. Concerned that televised close-ups of the ball might show the NFL logo during college games, the NCAA banned balls bearing professional league logos from use in NCAA games in 1986, a standard that continues today.

A final note about branding and gridiron footballs has been that football has largely avoided the distinctive branding graphics seen in other sports. An upstart professional football league or two might have dolled up the ball with orange stripes or other distinct markings. Still, football has not gone the route of the American Basketball Association's red, white, and blue basketball or the commonplace use of graphics and distinctly colored panels on soccer balls, rugby balls, volleyballs, and international basketball. The same is true of Gaelic and Australian Rules football. Teams in those sports do not play matches with plain leather balls.

Other than the NFL imprinting a new game logo on Super Bowl balls each year, football has otherwise stuck close to its knitting, using tan balls, with or without white stripes. Presumably, the impact of designs on the quarterback's grip is the primary contributor to staying true to the old-school leather appearance.

**Summary**

Five historical influences have shaped the coloring and striping of today's footballs. The first four influences reflected the functional needs of players on the field, while the fifth and most recent reflects the marketing or branding value of balls that appear distinctive.

Footballs were initially covered with leather because it was the best material and readily available centuries before artificial fabrics and other materials arrived. Leather remains the primary football covering today.

The desire to practice and play football under artificial light led to the painting of footballs and later to the tanning of the leather in lighter colors so players and fans could see the ball under the poor artificial lighting of the time.

This visibility need, combined with the desire to counter the camouflaging of the brown or white ball against uniforms, led to striping the ball. Sporting goods manufacturers variously placed one or more stripes toward the ends of the ball, with the location and number differing until the football world settled on one stripe on each end that did not intersect with the lacing. Painted balls and the location of stripes that interfered with the passer's grip have led to designs that eliminate the stripes or place them only on the ball's top panels.

Of course, improved lighting conditions make the stripes largely unnecessary, but they remain on many footballs, primarily to provide a distinctive look for different leagues and levels of play.

Unlike other sports that churn through distinctively covered balls, football has stayed true to the traditional tan leather covering. The presence and type of striping are now the primary visual methods to distinguish one league's ball from another's.

Overall, changes in the ball's appearance over time primarily resulted from functional requirements. Football experimented with various design solutions in response to changing functional requirements but has settled on appearance conventions that saw only one challenger in the last 50 years.

# 4

# MATERIALS AND MANUFACTURING

Football manufacturing began in the 1820s in England in shops owned by the sort of men seen in *The Christmas Carol* or other Dickens novels. In addition to shoes and boots, they crafted highly-quality leather rugby and soccer balls.

After American football broke from rugby, they no longer needed to use English rugby balls, so they switched to balls made in America by Spalding of Chicago. Spalding produced balls in large quantities in factories and matched the volume with a national distribution system. Soon, Spalding offered products in every sport imaginable, and as the market for sporting goods products grew, Spalding and its competitors became good-sized businesses.

Most early sporting goods firms and their suppliers came out of the meatpacking or leather industries since leather was the core material used for footballs and football equipment generally. The industry transitioned after WWII toward plastics and other synthetic materials, so many firms entering the industry since then have originated in those industries.

As we will see in this chapter, rubber and plastic footballs competed with leather for several decades, seeking to become the dominant football cover. Still, leather held them off and remains the unrivaled cover for footballs today.

**Pigskin, Sheepskin, Horsehide, and Cowhide**

In the 1860s and 1870s, the English used the term "pigskin" to describe polo and steeplechase saddles, not rugby or soccer balls. Americans adopted "pigskin" as a nickname for the ball and the game more broadly by the mid-1880s despite the rugby balls imported from England having rubber bladders by the time American colleges began playing organized football.

It is a common belief that cowhide or steerhide have covered footballs from the beginning. While largely accurate, sheepskin, horsehide, and pigskin once covered lower-priced footballs as well. The 1898 advertisement below includes a 75-cent sheepskin ball, while the highest-priced ball, a cowhide-covered Spalding, sold for $4.00.

*The first item listed is a 75-cent sheepskin football. ('Marshall Field & Co., Football Supplies,* Chicago Tribune, *November 7, 1898.)*

Sheepskin balls regularly appeared in ads as a lower-priced option until WWI. They were so inexpensive that boys' clothing retailers often gave them away to anyone purchasing a boys' suit or coat. There are pre-1900 ads for inexpensive "pigskin footballs" as well, though it is unclear whether the ads refer to the leather, the bladder, or are simply a redundancy. In addition, Wilson used elk leather for their late 1930s and early

1940s white footballs, presumably because elk leather was lighter-colored.

**WRW WHITE LEATHER WILSON OFFICIAL FOOTBALL.** This ball is official in every respect and has the same design and special features as the WR Football. The only difference is that the WRW is made of pebble grain white elk leather, which makes it suitable for night play. 8.50 Each $11.35

Black rings on white leather balls. .60 Each Ball $0.80

*The item description mentions that Wilson's white ball was made of elk leather. (1940 Wilson Football Catalog)*

Nevertheless, cowhide, specifically the hide of steers, has been the predominant football covering. English rugby and early American balls used split cowhide covers due to regular cowhide being too thick and heavy for balls. Cobblers and sporting goods manufacturers skived or split the leather to reduce its weight, using the outer layer with the grain for footballs. Moreover, since the leather grain is tighter along the animal's back and near the tail, higher-quality balls traditionally use leather only from those sections, while panels cut from other sections of the hide become lower-priced balls.

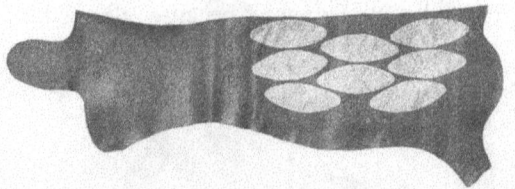

Please notice the picture of the trimmed back, which originally came from an American steer. See how little of it can actually be used in the Official 5R Foot Ball. The other parts of the skin not cut away are those used for the cheaper grades of Foot Balls.

*The image and caption show the portions of a steer hide used for footballs. (1922-1923 D&M Fall & Winter Catalog)*

Early footballs were unlined, comprising only the bladder, leather casing, and potential reinforcing around the laces. The structural integrity of animal bladders and, later, leather-covered rubber bladders was problematic, so the hide was stretched before the panels were cut, hoping they would not stretch further during play. The tightly sewn panels helped maintain the ball's shape, but GoldSmith, which produced unlined balls as late as 1925, only guaranteed their top football for two games or the equivalent practice use.

### *The Two Game Guarantee*

The Goldsmith Official Collegiate Foot Balls Nos. RS and F5 are made of the finest quality English Tempered Hide and are guaranteed to retain their shape for two full games. We do not guarantee against variation in size, shape and weight for more than two games or its equivalent amount of use in practice.

*(1925-26 GoldSmith Athletic Equipment, Fall & Winter)*

Much of the durability problem stemmed from leather's propensity to absorb moisture, become heavier, and expand, making punting and kicking difficult. Balls sometimes became so waterlogged that they expanded to the point that their laces snapped, leading to the demand for stronger laces and less absorbent leather.

Manufacturers claimed to have licked the waterlogged ball problem since they started making footballs. For example, Wright & Ditson claimed in 1889 that their English Rugby "Match" Foot Ball was:

> ...made of a special grade of leather, each section of which is separately dressed in such a way that it is waterproof, and a perfect shape is guaranteed, which will be retained in all weathers.[1]

Technological advances and greater emphasis on the passing game led football manufacturers to pursue less water-absorbent balls. Whether manufacturers tanned the leather differently or impregnated it with secret substances, they claimed their balls were water-resistant or waterproof.

The 1927-28 GoldSmith Fall and Winter catalog proclaimed:

> The waterproofing is a distinct advantage. It makes the ball imperious to water and prevents it from getting heavy or soggy on a wet day.[2]

The demand for reduced water absorption continued. By 1940, GoldSmith, the same manufacturer as above, claimed their ball was not just water-repellant but waterproof. The same catalog described a test in which footballs were submerged in water for a specified time, with the treated GoldSmith ball gaining only one-quarter ounce in weight while untreated balls gained 4 1/8 ounces. Who knows what was real, but water resistance or waterproofing was a desired product feature.

*GoldSmith's water test is described at the bottom of the page. (1940 GoldSmith Preferred Sports Equipment Fall & Winter)*

MacGregor, which purchased GoldSmith in 1940, claimed its 1949 leather was scientifically tanned for a better grip and waterproofed by a newly developed process. The claim was mainly marketing spin, but it reflected a football world that wanted more reliable, less water-absorbent footballs. So, while leather football manufacturers looked for ways to reduce water absorbency, an old competitor reemerged, seeking to tear the leather football market asunder.

## Rubber Footballs Bounce Back

As mentioned earlier, round rubberized American balls gained popularity in the mid-1800s. However, once American college students adopted rugby as their game, they played using an oval, leather-covered rugby ball. The American rubberized ball remained on the market and may have gained use in soccer or other games, but rubberized balls of all shapes mainly saw use in playground and backyard games.

At least, that was the case until the 1930s, when Voit started selling rubber footballs as a substitute for leather balls in varsity competitions. Other manufacturers sold rubber balls post-WWII, but Voit was the segment pioneer and primary promoter.

Most traditional sporting goods manufacturers began life in the meat packing and leather industries. Voit started as a materials manufacturer for the tire retreading market, later turning to rubber balls. Voit's rubber balls received extensive use for recreational purposes by American troops during WWII, and the story goes that they proved more durable than leather footballs at rest stations in the humid conditions of the Pacific Theater. In addition, the war spurred significant investment in synthetic rubber research, production, and applications, so Voit's products likely improved after the war. Whatever circumstances contributed to their success, Voit was taken seriously as a football supplier post-war.

Rubber footballs quickly gained popularity among high schools in the Pacific Northwest. The Oregon High School Coaches Association approved rubber footballs for games in 1948, while the NFHS selected schools nationwide to test rubber balls in 1950.

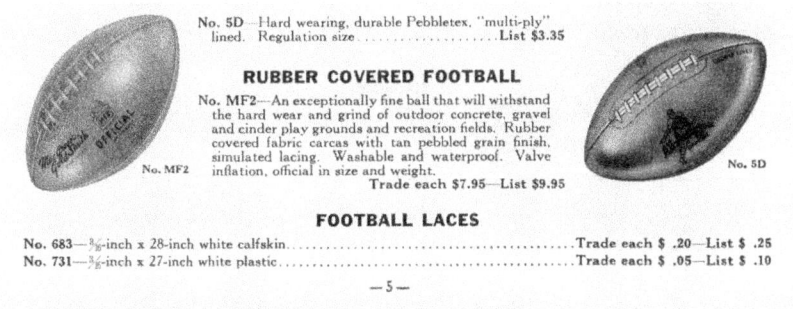

*While MacGregor GoldSmith sold rubber footballs in 1948, they positioned them for playground use rather than the varsity fields. (1948 Fall and Winter MacGregor GoldSmith Catalog)*

Rubber had several advantages over leather, being more durable and water-repellant. In addition, many players thought rubber retained its grip better, leading to improved quarterback accuracy and reduced fumbling. At least, that was the pitch.

Voit aggressively marketed the balls, promoting their use in test games. Georgia Tech coach Bobby Dodd was among those on Voit's advisory panel and was paid to promote the rubber ball across the South, so it is no surprise that the first major college game to use a rubber football was the 1951 Georgia Tech-Louisiana State game. A few small college teams on the West Coast used it, as did Hofstra and Kings Point in their 1951 game. The Voit push won over UCLA coach Red Sanders, who predicted the leather football and basketball would be "as rare as a raw steak" in a few years.[3]

Over 1,000 high school games used Voit's XF9 ball in 1951. Rubber balls got a big break when the NFHS approved their use in 1952, provided both teams agreed to its use. However, coaches who didn't like rubber balls refused to use them when requested, so the NFHS revised the rule for 1954 to allow each team's offense to use the regulation ball of their choosing, initiating a practice that is now standard.

Likewise, the NCAA regulations went from:

> 1952: "...ball made of other materials may be used at mutual agreement of the contesting teams."[4]

> 1956: "A rubber-covered ball may be used at mutual agreement of the contesting teams, or by election of either team while on offense."[5]

> 1957: "A rubber-covered ball may be used at mutual agreement of the contesting teams."[6]

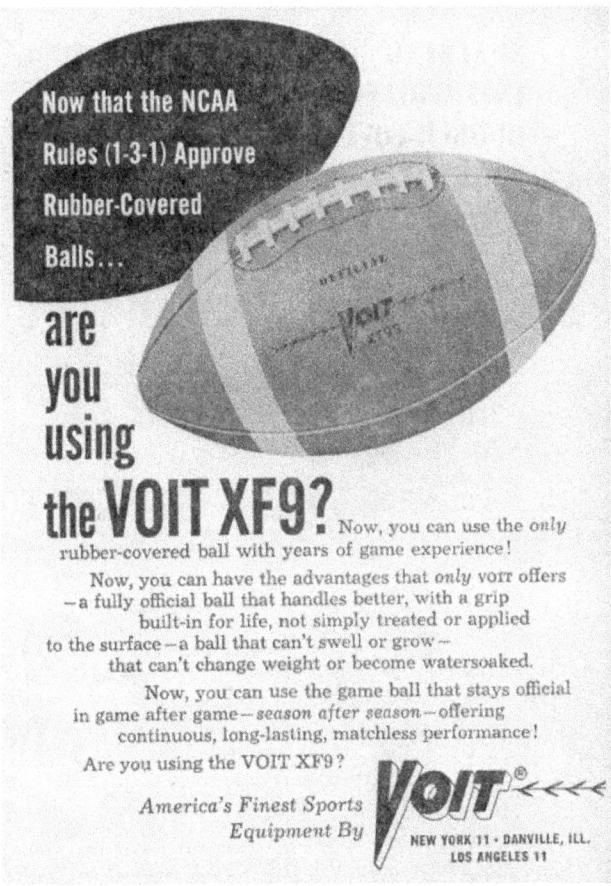

*A Voit XF9 advertisement from 1956. (Official NCAA Football Guide. New York: National Collegiate Athletic Bureau. 1956. With Permission of Voit USA)*

The rubber footballs' early success led many to think they would replace their leather cousins by 1960, just as rubber had replaced leather for most basketballs, soccer balls, and volleyballs. Of course, it did not turn out that way, but people at all levels of football seriously considered the idea.

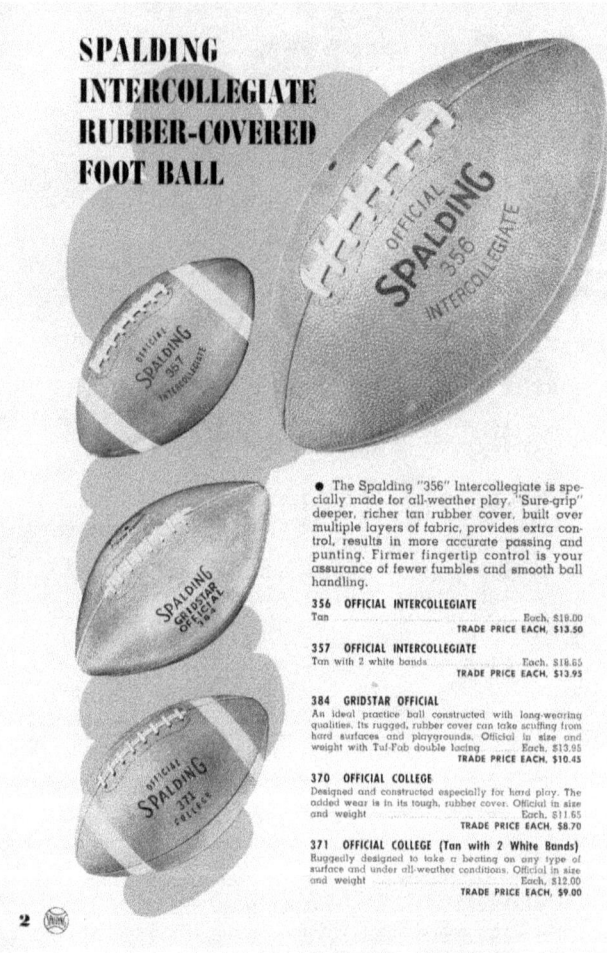

(1955 Spalding Catalog)

The percentage of rubber versus leather football usage is difficult to trace. Still, rubber footballs continued to be used at all levels of college football throughout the 1980s, primarily in games played in the rain. However, the NCAA returned to allowing leather footballs only in 1993. By then, teams could use multiple balls during games, and most played on artificial turf or well-drained grass fields that limited the balls' exposure to water and mud.

Composite leather balls arrived in the 1990s. Composite leather is analogous to fiberboard, consisting of ground leather scraps bonded with polyurethane, with the percentage of leather versus polyurethane varying by application. Substantially less expensive than leather balls, composite leather balls are illegal in college and pro games but are common in youth leagues and as practice balls at higher levels. Among the challenges composite balls face is that they become slippery when wet, but their lower costs make them competitive with leather for some applications.

**Getting a Grip**

Players have fumbled footballs since their rugby days, so concerns about gripping the ball are longstanding. One method of enhancing the ball's grip has been using pebbled or pebble-grain leather. Leather industry lore tells us pebbling originated by accident when a Scotch tanner of the early 1800s left a tall stack of leather on a stony floor for several weeks. When it came time to use the leather at the bottom of the pile, the tanner noticed the leather had taken on a pebbled texture, which he and others sought to reproduce. Using pressure and heat to emboss leather became a standard practice among tanners and leatherworkers, though its purpose is decorative for most applications.

Football lacks an origin story regarding the first use of pebble-grain leather. Advertisements for Lillywhite and other early rugby balls indicate they were made of English grain leather but did not mention pebbling. Advertisements for footballs made with pebbled leather appeared by 1896.

('Rugby Football,' St. Louis Post-Dispatch, October 4, 1907.)

Although football manufacturers likely pursued methods to enhance the balls' grip, their pursuit did not become a selling point in their catalogs or advertisements until rubber footballs arrived in the 1940s.

MacGregor GoldSmith's 1946 catalog touted their ball's "tacky finish for better passing and ball handling.[7] They made the same claim in 1955 but couched it as part of their Tac-Touch method of treating leather. Meanwhile, Rawlings relied on their Formula-15 treatment in 1956 and a process providing the "Slow-Drag" feel in 1959.

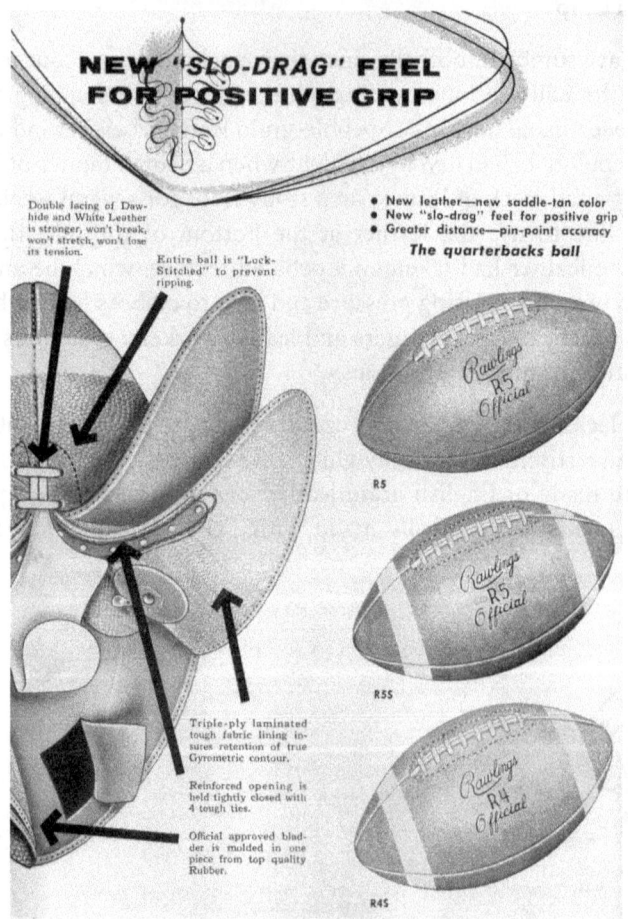

*(1959-60 Rawlings Fall & Winter Catalog)*

It is now difficult to determine whether the various processes produced substantive differences in the leather or were essentially marketing tactics. However, the 1950s process that has had the longest-lasting impact was the tanning process developed by Horween Leather of Chicago, founded in 1905 by Isadore Horween, a Ukrainian immigrant.

Two of Isadore's sons, Ralph and Arnold, played football at Harvard before joining the Racine and Chicago Cardinals in the early 1920s. Arnold was the Cardinals' player-coach in 1923 and 1924, in addition to coaching Harvard from 1926 to 1930, after which he joined the family firm.

Meanwhile, George Halas, the Chicago Bears owner, helped another Chicago-based company, Wilson Sporting Goods, become the exclusive supplier of footballs to the NFL in 1941. Halas, whose Bears beat the Cardinals all three times the teams met when he and Arnold were opposing player coaches, approached his old rival in the late 1940s, asking if he could improve the leather used for NFL footballs. Horween already tanned leather for Wilson, but the request led Arnold Horween to develop the Grip-Tite process, which improved the leather's grip, limited moisture absorption, and helped the pebbling last longer.

Wilson showcased Horween's Grip-Tite leather in advertisements for baseball gloves in 1953 and then for golf grips and basketballs. Wilson field-tested Grip-Tite footballs in 1954, and by 1955, the leather came into use for NFL balls, with the Grip-Tite name branded on the Duke balls. Wilson also touted Grip-Tite in the description of their non-NFL balls, so it was not a process exclusive to the NFL.

*Grip-Tite appears in the description of all but the junior ball shown on this catalog page. (Wilson Fall Winter Catalog, 1956-57 Trade Price Edition)*

Whether due to a process change or not, the leather for NFL balls gained the Tanned in Tack® name by the 1966 season, when it appeared in comparisons of NFL and American Football League balls. The comparisons noted that the grip or tackiness of the NFL ball was tanned into the leather, whereas the AFL's Spalding ball had its tackiness sprayed on.

By either name, Horween has been Wilson's exclusive leather supplier for NFL balls since 1955. It also sells other leather to Wilson and its competitors.

## Stickum

If Grip-Tite and Tanned in Tack® were not enough, some players thought using substances to enhance their grip was necessary. As far back as 1893, Yale's players applied resin to their hands after learning Harvard planned to wear leather uniforms in their game. Cecil Cushman, the longtime coach at the University of Redlands, developed a sticky or tacky substance called "Stickum" to help his ball handlers catch in the 1930s.

Still, Stickum was seldom a problem until 1977 when Lester Hayes, a rookie cornerback with the Oakland Raiders, was introduced to the product by his teammate, Fred Biletnikoff. Hayes soon applied Stickum to his hands in such quantity that opposing players complained it affected their ability to snap, throw, and otherwise handle the ball. The excessive Stickum era ended when the NFL banned sticky and slippery substances in 1981. The subsequent rise of receivers' grip-enhancing gloves has reduced gripping concerns for all positions other than quarterback.

## The Grip Enhanced Football

We covered Charles Finley's Visually Enhanced Ball in Chapter 3, and he also made noise with the Grip Enhanced Football, which made a dent in the football grip challenge. The Grip Enhanced Football aimed to improve the quarterback's grip and spin, reduce fumbling, and enhance the receiver's ability to catch the ball while it also flew farther.

The secret to the Grip Enhanced Football was the leather produced by Horween Leather, which provides the leather for NFL footballs. Rather than having a raised pebble grain, grip-enhanced leather had small dimples or indentations, like a golf ball.

"Golf ball dimples" are featured on Charlie Finley's latest innovation that he hopes will improve football for players and fans.

*A detailed view of the dimpled leather of a Grip Enhanced Football. ('Finley Gets Grip On Footballs,' Indianapolis News, September 6, 1990.)*

The Grip Enhanced Ball received NCAA approval in October 1990, with Michigan being an early adopter. Finley, it turns out, had met Bo Schembechler through baseball because Schembechler became the Detroit Tigers' president after leaving Michigan. Bo connected Finley with the Wolverine's equipment manager, who became intrigued by the ball and promoted its use internally.

Michigan used the ball for the remainder of the 1990 regular season and in its Gator Bowl appearance. Eight other teams used the ball during the 1990-1991 bowl games, though they all appear to have used the Grip Enhanced Football with standard college striping - transverse stripes on the two panels adjacent to the laces and no stripes on the bottom panels.

It is unknown how many teams used the Grip Enhanced Football in 1991, but Michigan used the ball and had a great season, losing only to #1 Florida State in the third game of the season and to #2 Washington in the Rose Bowl. Elevating the ball's status was quarterback Elvis Grbac, who led the NCAA in passing efficiency, and Desmond Howard, who won the

Heisman Trophy after scoring 19 touchdowns on pass receptions, including one or two of the circus variety.

While Michigan's 1991 season might have convinced others to appreciate the value of dimples, only Wyoming, Kent State, and Rice joined the Wolverines in using the ball in 1992 before the Grip Enhanced Football encountered two problems. One came when Rawlings, who produced the ball, asked the courts to invalidate Finley's patent, claiming that Finley did not invent the dimpled leather. (We will cover the tannery story shortly.) The legal disputes with Finley made Rawlings reluctant to promote or produce the ball.

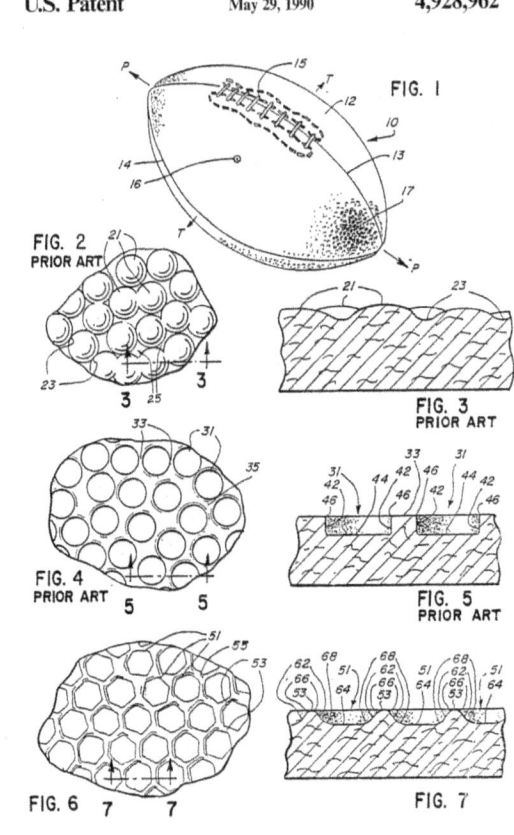

*Drawings from U.S. Patent 4,928,962 issued to Charles O. Finley on May 29, 1990.*

The second problem came in November 1992 when Michigan hosted Illinois on a cold and snowy Ann Arbor day. The Grip Enhanced Ball became noticeably stiffer and slicker than the traditional pebbled ball and received blame for Michigan's 17 fumbles, interceptions, dropped balls, and botched PAT holds that day. At the same time, Illinois had one mishandled ball using a pebbled ball. Michigan used the Grip Enhanced Football the following week versus Ohio State without incident. However, they returned to the traditional pebbled ball as they avenged their 1992 Rose Bowl loss to Washington by beating them in the 1993 Grandaddy.

Like the Visually Enhanced Ball, the Grip Enhanced Football or "Double Grip" ball quickly faded from public view and the product disappeared from the market.

Since then, football manufacturers have continued treating leather or applying substances to help players achieve the perfect grip. Football teams now customize game balls to their quarterbacks' preferences rather than accept the balls arriving from the factory as is.

For example, before 2006, the NFL's home team submitted 24 balls per game. However, since 2006, home and visiting teams have submitted twelve balls per game for use by their offense. The procedure allows each team to treat the balls with a mixture of secret sauces to meet their quarterback's approval. Wilson supplies twelve factory-fresh balls, or "K balls," to the officials for the kicking game.

**Lining**

Footballs are subjected to tremendous forces when punted, kicked, and otherwise knocked about the field and are especially prone to become misshapen when wet. While the football world focuses on the ball's leather or rubber exterior, stripes, and valves, modern footballs retain their shape due to their underappreciated linings. From the early days, preparing leather included stretching the hide and panels to minimize changes to the ball's shape during use on the field.

Early footballs consisted only of the bladder, leather cover, stitching, and lacing. However, the leather's flexibility led manufacturers to sew liners onto the leather panels to help them retain their shape. Reach used canvas liners in 1918, and D&M went without liners in 1921. GoldSmith promoted their unlined ball as traveling farther on kicks and punts, though they soon switched directions and began using and promoting their lining. The 1928 D&M catalog extolled how its "Du-Ply Cord Woven Lining, a D&M exclusive, prevents stretching and insures a perfect shaped ball."[8] Likewise, GoldSmith devoted an entire page to its "Zig-zag" stitched "Rhinotex" dual-ply lining in 1931.

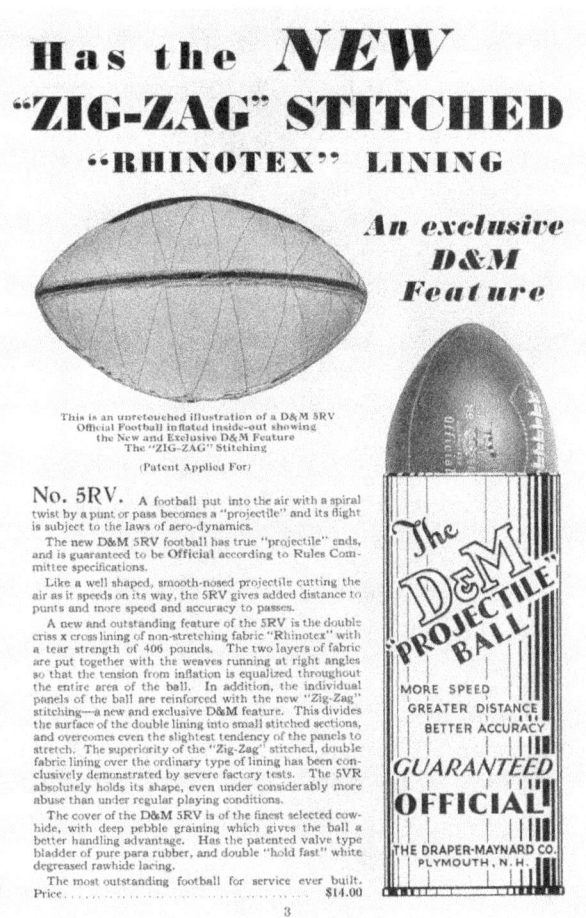

*The inner lining made an important contribution to the Projectile Ball. (1931-1932 D&M Athletic Goods Fall & Winter)*

Lining balls proved helpful, and by the late 1940s, footballs were triple-lined, an approach that continues today. The 1964 Rawlings catalog included a drawing highlighting their ball's construction, including its triple-ply herringbone lining.

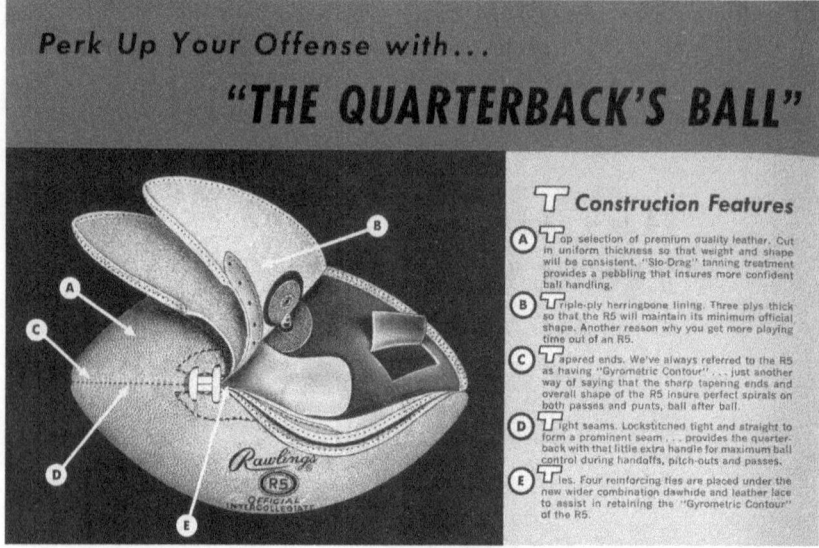

*A section of the 1964 Rawlings catalog details and materials used to construct a football. (1964 Rawlings Fall & Winter Catalog)*

Football manufacturers have continued improving the liners to limit deformations, but few notice their effects, so the discussion turns to more visible issues.

**Two, Four, and Eight-Panel Balls**

As the ball's size and profile became increasingly specified, sporting goods manufacturers looked for other methods to improve the ball's performance. An approach that emerged in the early 1930s was to change the number of panels on the ball's leather cover. The standard football then and now has four panels of equal shape and size: two on the top adjacent to the laces and two on the bottom.

However, rugby balls have had four, six, and eight panels over the years. The awareness of rugby ball panels may have led American manufacturers to experiment with the number of panels on a football, and they soon claimed the eight-section or panel ball with seven seams improved the passer's grip and helped the ball sail through the air more reliably, akin to an arrow's fletching.

*Rawlings eight-section balls of 1934. (1934-1935 Rawlings Fall and Winter Sports Catalog)*

The availability of an eight-section ball created a minor controversy at the start of the 1931 season. However, the balls conformed to the NCAA specifications regarding the ball's length, circumference, and inflation level, so they continued in use. The NCAA clarified the issue in the 1932 rules, noting that balls with more than four sections were legal as long as both teams approved their use.

Not to be outdone, the thought leaders at Reach Wright & Ditson went the opposite direction by producing a two-panel ball, which they also claimed flew better than a four-panel ball. Sometimes referred to as the rabbit ball, they put the laces in the middle of the top panel and eliminated the seam on the ball's bottom to allow for more accurate punting. They also shifted seams so they did not meet at the ball's nose, providing a less erratic bounce on dropkicks.

Page 2        **REACH OFFICIAL FOOT BALLS**

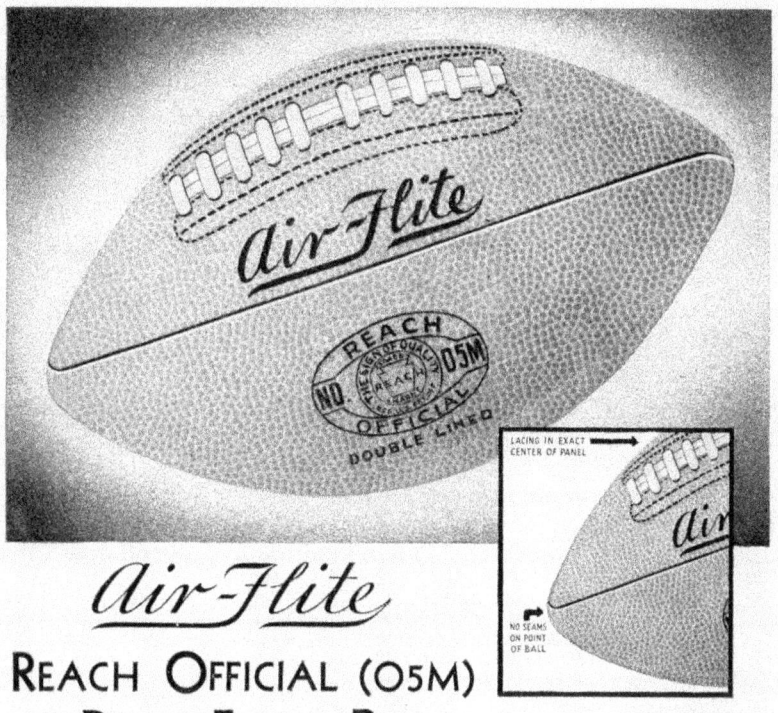

## Reach Official (O5M) 2-Piece Foot Ball

**GREATER ACCURACY
LONGER PUNTS
LASTING SHAPE**

A new type of foot ball both in design and construction. Air-Flite is made with only two sections of leather eliminating the four seamed ends necessary in the four piece ball—thereby affording greater and more evenly balanced air capacity.

With the lacing in center of top panel the opposite panel presents a perfect kicking surface due to the elimination of the center seam. The kick is made on an unbroken surface of the panel resulting in greater accuracy.

The shape of the Air-Flite, due to the position of the seams and the smooth ends, affords a surer grip for more accurate passing.

The Air-Flite balances more accurately when it lands on its nose because of its smooth ends—a decided advantage on drop and place kicks.

Constructed of specially tanned, selected grade Reach pebbled-grained Tuf-ide leather. Double lined, double laced and equipped with our new patented rubber valve bladder that is absolutely leak proof—there is no possibility of accidental puncture while inflating. Each ball is inflated and carefully inspected before it leaves our factory. Approved as an official ball for 1934 by the Rules Committee............Each, **$12.85**

*For Other Air-Flite Foot Balls, see Pages 4 and 5 • For Policy Notice, see Page 3.*

*Reach produced the 2-piece "rabbit" ball in 1934. (1934 Fall 1935 Winter Reach Wright & Ditson Catalog)*

Another variation on the theme was Goldsmith's Multiple Seam ball. Constructed with the standard four panels, each panel had an additional stitched seam running almost the length of each panel. Like the eight-panel ball, the multiple-seam ball purportedly enhanced the ball's ability to sail through the air. However, the ball violated the NCAA's specifications prohibiting "corrugations" or grooves other than those for the seams and laces. In addition, few noticed a performance difference, and the ball sailed off the shelves and into football's dustbin.

The Multiple Seam ball failed to meet the NCAA specs regarding corrugation.(1935-36 GoldSmith Athletic Equipment, Fall & Winter)

## Manufacturing Footballs

Despite the many technological advances the world has witnessed since William Gilbert stitched his first rugby ball, the core processes used to make footballs have seen limited change. Footballs are made of leather and other pliable materials, making the automation of many manufacturing processes difficult. Workers in Gilbert's shop would recognize most of the steps used at Wilson's manufacturing plant in Ada, Ohio, which produces a good portion of today's footballs. The Ada plant has football's most widely publicized manufacturing process today, mainly due to it making the NFL's football for decades. Ada's contribution to the game results in an annual migration of beat writers visiting the plant and publishing human interest stories in the run-up to the Super Bowl.

Of course, making footballs does not begin at a football factory. Instead, it starts with cattle raised on a farm or ranch. The selected few go to a slaughterhouse, where their hides are pulled from their carcasses and cured in salt for ten days before being sent to the Horween tannery, which has provided the leather for NFL footballs since 1955.

After arriving at the tannery, the cured hides are trimmed, dehaired, bated, and pickled before being soaked in water and tannins during the tanning process. The resulting leather is stretched, retanned, dyed, and pebbled based on the intended use. Horween sends some of its finest sporting goods leather to Rawlings for use in Major League Baseball gloves. The leather sent to Wilson for NFL balls needs to be tougher because it serves a different function. Nevertheless, the leather is processed to exacting standards regardless of its destination.

The slaughtering, curing, and tanning processes that produce leather for footballs are less labor intensive than in the old days, but not by much. The same is true of the manufacturing process for footballs, which is classic factory work, broken into one hundred or so steps executed at a series of stations. The process begins at the cutting station, where the ball's four panels are die-cut from a hide. Those four panels stay together to become a ball. The panels enter a machine that stamps logos, foils, or artwork on the panel exterior before entering a splitting machine to shave excess leather from the panels' undersides so each weighs nearly the same. The split leather panels then move to a station where they are lined.

*Adding liners to the ball helped reduce stretched and misshapen leather panels. ('Footballs Are Not Made Of Pigskin, As Generally Believed, But Calfskin,' Brooklyn Daily Eagle, November 5, 1911.)*

In addition to liners, they sew reinforcing strips in place and punch holes on the top panels that will receive lacing several steps down the line.

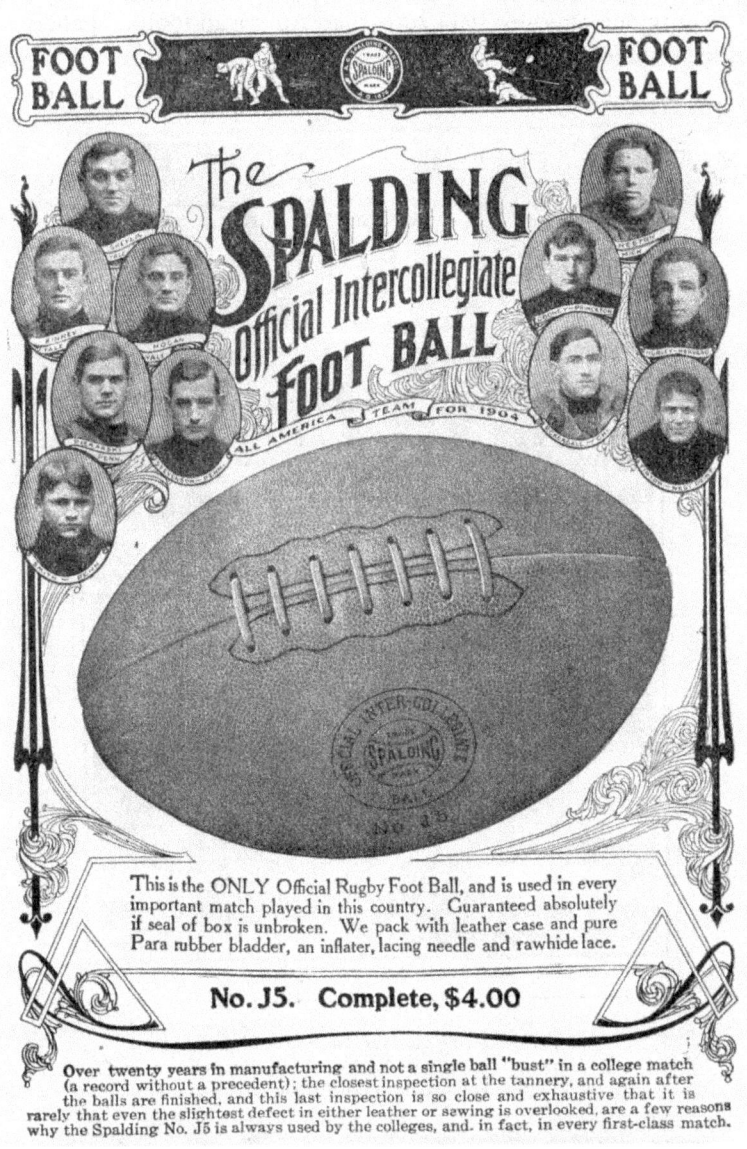

*The stitches for the reinforcing strips that support the punched holes and lacing are evident in the picture of the 1905 Spalding J5. (1905-1906 Spalding Fall & Winter)*

Next, the top and bottom quarter panels are sewn together before the halves are stitched inside out. The lock stitching is hand-guided but machine-sewn. In 1892, the RFU specified that rugby balls had to be hand-stitched, but the folks on the west side of the Atlantic did not have that requirement, and by 1911 or earlier, American football panels were machine-stitched.

Stitching the Seams.

*Using powered sewing machines to make footballs became the American way. ('Footballs Are Not Made Of Pigskin, As Generally Believed, But Calfskin,'* Brooklyn Daily Eagle, *November 5, 1911.)*

After being sewn, the balls are turned, the manufacturing process's most physically demanding step. Turners place the inside-out leather shell onto a metal post and manually turn the cover outside in so the leather, rather than the liner, is on the outside.

After turning, the lacer stuffs a bladder into the ball, pushes the inflation bung through its pre-punched hole, and hand-laces it. Finally, the ball moves to the molding station, where it is placed in a mold and inflated to 120 psi, giving the pigskin its final shape. Balls in the mold were only inflated to 60 pounds in 1960, which tells us today's bladders are stronger, and other tolerances are tighter.

After reducing the inflation level to 13 psi, the ball moves on to the quality control process for final trimming, inspection, and grading. Only the highest-quality balls are sent to NFL teams for game use, while the remainder are sold at retail.

Non-NFL balls made by Wilson undergo similar processes, but differences in specifications require slightly different procedures, such as painting or sewing the stripes on balls.

**Summary**

Despite attempts to replace pebbled leather with rubber, reverse pebbling, or composite leather, the game has stayed true to its leather origins. Nevertheless, there have been times when people at the top of the game seriously considered and used materials other than leather for the game's ball. It is a frightening thought and altogether expected.

After all, the football is no more sacred than players' pads or shoes or the grass fields upon which the game is still sometimes played. Leather was an essential material in the game's first century. It was the primary material for helmets, shoulder pads, shoes, and other football equipment. The increased use of foam rubber in the 1920s, synthetic fabrics and plastics in the 1950s, and other materials have since taken leather's place for other football equipment, so it is conceivable that another substance could have replaced leather in the past or will do so in the future.

However, leather has weathered the storms to remain the primary material used in the game's balls. It fended off rubber from the 1940s until 1993. Had George Halas not asked Arnie Horween to look into improving football leather, today's balls might be made of a different material, like most inflated balls worldwide. Whether marketed under the Grip-Tite or Tanned-in-Tack names, an underappreciated tannery in Chicago managed to hold back the tide of alternative football covers.

Beyond the football cover, the Wilson-NFL alliance has made significant contributions to the game of football. Neither entity changed the ball's shape or size. The ball used by the NFL today is the same size as the NCAA set in 1934 and the NFL copied in 1935. The NFL ball's white cover and stripes have come and gone. Still, the most critical effect of the

Wilson-NFL alliance has been their focus on the ball's reliability, consistency, and manufacturing quality. The uniformity of the footballs used in NFL games results from that focus, and those quality control procedures carry over to the balls Wilson produces for other leagues and markets, as well as their competitors.

# 5

# GAME AND PRACTICE FOOTBALLS

Since footballs were first produced and sold commercially, their makers have sold balls of varying quality and pricing. Often, customers purchased the highest-quality balls for use in match play because they wanted to avoid problems with the ball that might affect the enjoyment or outcome of games. In contrast, lower-quality and less expensive balls were used in practice, by lower-level teams, or in backyard play.

So, we will first cover game balls and the traditions and practices surrounding their use before moving to special-purpose footballs produced for training and practice rather than gameplay.

**Game Balls**

The NFL uses up to 36 footballs per game. Each team submits twelve balls they have prepared to meet their quarterbacks' tackiness and other preferences. The officiating crew inspects the team-submitted balls before the game to ensure they comply with league standards, following each team's secret sauce preparations. In addition, Wilson sends twelve balls straight from the factory for use on kicking plays. Kicking or K-balls entered the game in 2007 after the NFL decided teams took too many liberties in selecting the balls used by kickers.

Using 36 footballs per game would seem preposterous to the game's old-timers, who treated game balls like sacred objects. By tradition and then by rule, early American football used one ball for the entire game. Football did not acquire its one-ball per-game tradition from rugby since rugby did not have such a rule. The Rugby School traditionally switched balls at halftime of big matches, but that tradition did not spread to the broader rugby community. Instead, the number of balls used per game was unspecified.

Top-quality footballs were treated as sacred objects in the 1800s, though they cost about the same as today in real dollars. At the time, lower-level schools might struggle to buy one or two high-quality footballs per year, but budgets were not the issue for elite Eastern colleges and other high-level teams. Ticket sales and alumni contributions paid for team travel, training table, and equipment expenses, so they had the money to buy more than one ball per game if they wanted.

So, why did they insist on using one ball? Using one ball matched football's original requirement that the starting fifteen or eleven play the entire game without substitutes. However, the more critical factor was likely the initial scarcity of rugby balls in North America rather than their price. This scarcity led to their treatment as objects of honor and symbols of a hard-fought victory for the winning team. The only ball used in a hard-fought win became an object worth venerating, a trophy.

*The 1896 Chicago-Purdue game ball is in archives of the Hanna Holborn Gray Special Collections Research Center at the University of Chicago. (UChicago Magazine, Spring 2019)*

It is unclear why the practice of awarding game balls originated, though it likely followed the tradition of seizing battle flags and equipment from defeated enemies as war trophies. Among the Eastern colleges, the home team supplied the game ball, with the home captain keeping the ball if his team won and awarding it to the opposing captain when the home team lost. That did not happen every time, as will be covered shortly.

Chapter 1 mentioned the All-Canada team awarding the game ball to Harvard, who gave it to Princeton, who presented it to Yale after losing their game in 1876. Another early mention of game balls came at Princeton's 1886 commencement, where they draped the rostrum with a banner and the "trophy football" to celebrate their 1885 victory over Yale.[1]

Six years later, an article reporting on Princeton's athletic clubhouse mentioned its trophy room, which included baseballs and footballs of its winning teams.

> ...the athletic clubhouse, one of the most magnificently appointed buildings of its kind in the country. There are within it sumptuous dressing rooms, with training tables for different teams. The diet is under medical supervision. The upper stories accommodate the "graduated coachers," who return and coach the team in season. There is of course a room for trophies. It contains the winning baseballs and football with banners and photographs of winning teams.[2]

While the winning team was supposed to leave the field with the game ball, that did not happen at times due to poor sportsmanship. A Yale player took the game ball after losing to Harvard in 1891, giving it to a spectator, who pierced it with a knife and secreted it from the stadium by hiding the deflated ball in a blanket. Feeling guilty, Yale sent the ball to Harvard several months later, though it still had a hole in its bladder. Similarly, after Princeton lost to Penn for the first time in 1892, Princeton took the ball from the field and cut it into pieces, so Penn never received the ball. In another example, a Harvard player kept the ball after losing to Penn in 1896 until the Harvard coach intervened and sent the ball to Penn.

*1912 Princeton-Dartmouth game ball (Division of Culture and the Arts, National Museum of American History, Smithsonian Institution)*

After those incidents, most everyone returned to their senses, and hosts graciously gave the game ball to the victors following losses and some ties. Offering the game ball after tie games sometimes led to disputes. One occurred in 1930 during Fritz Crisler's first season coaching Minnesota, when they tied a favored Stanford team 0-0. As the coaches met on the field after the game, Crisler offered the ball to Stanford coach Pop Warner. The irascible Warner refused to accept it, suggesting an alternate location where Crisler should stick the ball.

The one-ball-per-game thing continued until 1917, despite balls getting wet, muddy, soggy, and heavy. Still, teams danced with the ball that brung them until the increased use of the forward pass led to a 1917 rules amendment to allow the use of a new ball at the start of the second half:

> In the case of a wet field, the ball may be changed for a new one at the end of the second period at the discretion of the Referee.[3]

Even then, it was unthinkable that the game might evolve such that ball boys would shuttle balls in and out of the game, drying them and removing mud. Yet, the NFL now uses 36 balls per game, which presents a marketing opportunity they can borrow from rugby. Rugby uses multiple game balls and now auctions them to whoever has the money to buy them, as occurred following the Rugby World Cup 2023.[4]

## Practice Balls

To this point, the discussion has ignored the distinction between balls intended for practice versus game use. Yet players spend far more time snapping, carrying, passing, and kicking footballs in practice than in games, so reviewing the historical attempts to create practice footballs makes sense. However, the reality is that there have been few attempts to develop footballs targeted for practice.

Some practice balls were former high-priced game balls that were no longer ready for prime time, but most were purchased for use in practice, so teams economized and bought lower-quality, less expensive balls. Every sporting goods catalog pitched their mid-priced balls as meeting the specifications, making them perfect for practice.

No. 5U

**No. 5U—"Interscholastic."** Regulation size. Durable American process cowhide lined with canvas. Heavy linen cord stitching. Especially suitable for practice. Complete with pure gray gum bladder, leather lace and lacing needle.....................Each, $7.00

GoldSmith's No. 5U was three dollars cheaper than their top ball and was touted as "especially suited for practice." (1925-26 Goldsmith Athletic Equipment, Fall & Winter)

In addition to the standard football used in practice, other practice balls strayed from the official specifications in ways that provided a training advantage—or at least, that was the thinking.

**Tethered Football**

Fred Gehrke, a former NFL player and coach, is best known for designing the horns for the Los Angeles Rams helmets in 1948, the first logo on professional football helmets. Later, while working with the Denver Broncos, Gehrke also designed the first sideline net used by kickers to warm up or practice during games. Gehrke's kicking net highlighted one of the challenges kickers and punters faced before his invention. That is, every time they kicked the ball downfield, they or someone else had to run downfield to shag the balls.

A few kickers and punters were smart enough to kick the ball into the nets or tarps hanging from the crossbars passers used for target practice. Others kicked into soccer goal nets.

*Passers throwing at targets in practice in 1925. (Harvard University, Harvard University Archives, W401856)*

But, football had a few tinkerers who developed solutions to the problems faced in practice and games. One attempt to address the kickers' problem came in the 1920s, when William J. Dolan, Jr. of Pearl River, New York, applied for a patent on his tethered football. Dolan filed for a patent in 1923, and his tethered football soon appeared in the 1925-1926 D&M Fall & Winter catalog.

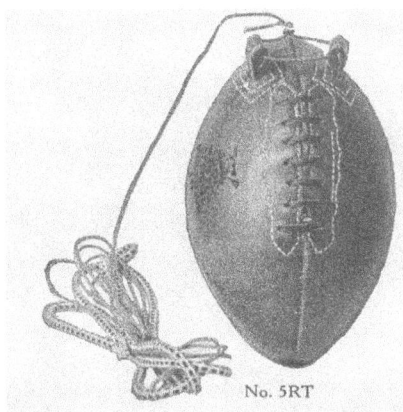

## D & M
## Tethered Football

No. 5RT. The Dolan patented tethered football.

This is a regulation football in every way, attached to a strong cord to which is fastened an elastic. This in turn can be fastened to a limb of a tree or to a goal post and brings the ball back every time. Any kind of a kick or a pass can be gotten away with this ball.

| | |
|---|---|
| Complete. | 12.00 |
| Ball alone. | 11.00 |
| Elastic and cord attachment. | 1.00 |

No. 5RT

*Dolan's tethered ball met regulations in every way except for the fasteners and cord. (1925-1926 D&M Fall & Winter Catalog)*

The catalog image and description indicate the kicker or passer could hang the tethered ball from a tree limb or goal post and kick or throw it to their heart's content, knowing the ball would travel only as far as the length of the cord.

While the tethered ball had limitations, it allowed kickers to kick more and walk less. However, like many other presumptive innovations, the tethered ball disappeared from the D&M catalog by 1928, so it does not appear to have been a big seller.

**Weighted Footballs**

While William Dolan, Jr. was a relative unknown, George Allen was a legendary NFL coach known for his attention to detail. Allen published the *Encyclopedia of Football Drills* while coaching the Whittier College Poets in 1954. Then, as Chicago Bears assistant in 1959, he published his *Complete Book of Winning Football Drills,* which includes over 500 drills covering every imaginable football situation.

In addition to being an author, Allen was an inventor and the creator of the game's first weighted football. Developed with Voit, they offered the Power Arm, weighing 19 ounces (versus the standard 14 to 15 ounces) and targeted for quarterbacks, and the 23-ounce Power Wrist ball for long snappers. Like weighted donuts on a baseball bat, the increased resistance offered by the heavier ball strengthened players' arms.

*A Power Arm training ball. (Courtesy of Ron Pomfrey)*

Weighted footballs gained popularity, with many top college and pro coaches touting their use. The Green Bay Packers' Bart Starr used one in training, as did various NFL and college quarterbacks into the mid-1980s. Thereafter, they have seen use by high school quarterbacks, though college and NFL quarterbacks occasionally mention using them in their past. Despite its use by some notable players and coaches, the weighted ball has seen intermittent use and has not significantly affected player training.

**Laceless Football**

When valves sitting flush with the ball's surface first appeared on inflated balls in the mid-1920s, the laces disappeared from nearly every inflated ball except the gridiron football. Footballs retained their laces because they aided those throwing forward passes using the overhand spiral technique.

With the recent emphasis on quarterbacks operating from the shotgun who need to throw the ball quickly on specific plays, Wilson and others began selling laceless footballs. Since there are no laces, the laceless ball helps break the quarterback's habit of rotating the ball to position the fingers on the laces. Of course, if quarterbacks no longer use the laces to throw the ball accurately, they will position their thumbs atop the painted stripes on half of their throws, resulting in a traumatic experience for some quarterbacks.

**Summary**

Rugby balls and footballs were relatively rare in the early days of rugby and football in North America. Few shops sold them, so they were treated as sacred objects based on their rarity rather than price. The Canadian All-Stars' awarding of game balls in their games with Harvard set a precedent for awarding game balls that continues today.

Despite football's 150-year history, few efforts have been made to develop training footballs. At least, there have been few efforts with enough promise that mainstream sporting goods manufacturers chose to sell the balls. The efforts behind tethered, weighted, and laceless footballs have largely been for naught. Each is seen as an oddity rather than an innovation.

Interestingly, no one has developed a meaningful football-based training device in the game's history, even in the 120 years since the forward pass became legal. That may be because throwing a football well is as much art as science. The future may give us virtual tools using footballs embedded with sensors to help develop quarterbacks, but those tools are not yet available.

# 6

# CONCLUSION

Footballs bridge the gap between life in the Middle Ages and today, taking shape in the mishmash of folk-kicking games that morphed into various regulated regional codes in the 1800s. As each regional game distinguished itself from its folk origins, the balls adapted to those circumstances, morphing over time and becoming less interchangeable. Today, you could play American football with a soccer ball, but you would not want to, and it would be far more challenging to play soccer with the ball used on the gridiron.

Although soccer and rugby balls have changed since the football codes began splitting in the mid-1860s, the gridiron football has experienced more significant change due to fundamental changes in the game itself. American football's early embrace of carrying the ball led to a preference for a smaller ball, and its adoption of the forward pass, which broke rugby's fundamental offside rule, led to the ball becoming more aerodynamic. The changes in the ball's shape were echoed when Canadian football made similar changes to its game.

### Changing the Ball's Shape and Size

The football's size and shape have varied, with the importance placed on the three methods of moving the ball: kicking, rushing, and passing. The football's original shape and size were a function of the size and shape of inflated animal bladders that were later covered with leather to make them more durable. While balls varied in size and shape, variations in local game rules led to preferences regarding the ball's shape. Those playing football at The Rugby School scored goals by kicking the ball over the crossbar, so they preferred ovalish rather than round balls. When the local cobblers received pigs' bladders that were more oval, they used them for their Rugby School customers, emphasizing the oval shape when covering those balls.

That dynamic changed with the invention of the rubber bladder because the ball's size and shape now resulted from a deliberate choice rather than random variations in pigs' bladders. Those balls were rounder than the prolate spheroid used today, but the more notable feature was their size, running 30 inches in circumference, or larger than a modern basketball. Balls of that size and shape worked well in games where the ball was kicked rather than carried. Although rugby allowed carrying the ball, it was primarily a kicking game until American preferences and rules of the 1870s and early 1880s led to an emphasis on carrying the ball. Rugby followed a similar path over the next decade.

By the 1880s, manufacturers offered English rugby, soccer, and other balls in sizes ranging from 30 to 18 inches. While American football started with 30-inch balls, the emphasis on carrying and possession led teams to use the easier-to-carry and retain 27-inch balls. This tendency became an official standard with the IFA's adoption of the Lillywhite Model J in 1886.

The continued desire for a smaller ball led Spalding to revise their Model J or J5 in 1903 to make it thinner and more aerodynamic. The 1903 change made the balls smaller and reshaped, so they were no longer rugby balls but had become footballs. While traditional wisdom indicates that the size of the ball changed in 1912, there is little evidence that this was the case. Instead, the 1912 football rules only formalized the size and shape used since 1903.

The development of the forward pass led to a desire for a smaller ball that could be more easily gripped and thrown by players, particularly those with smaller hands. Some manufacturers produced smaller than regulation balls, and their use in games led the NCAA to revise their specifications in 1929 and 1934. Besides a minor reduction in 1982, the football's size and shape have been unchanged since 1934. Still, over the course of the game's history, the football's shape changed as the game was reshaped.

## Changes in Construction

Along with changes in the ball's size and shape, there have been numerous changes in the materials used to construct the ball. The pig's bladder gave way to a leather-covered pig's bladder, then a leather-covered rubber bladder, and, eventually, a leather-covered urethane bladder. Each step in that process produced a more reliable ball.

Other enhancements in the ball's usability and durability came from adding linings to keep the natural leather from stretching, particularly when wet. The 1920s addition of valves that sat flush with the surface meant that most footballs went through life without unlaced and relaced. They were laced in the factory, and that was that.

While valves made life easier for the nation's equipment managers, they also allowed the football world to control and regulate the ball's inflation. Valves enabled the 1929 rule specifying the ball's inflation level so footballs could no longer be too hard or soft; they had to be just right.

The growth of the forward pass increased the desire to play with footballs that were not waterlogged and maintained their grips, even in wet and muddy conditions. Unable to rely on the footballs of the day to provide reassurance, football's rule-makers did the next best thing in 1917 when they changed the game's rules to give the referee the discretion to use a new ball in the second half of the game if needed.

Other improvements in the football came from enhancing the leather cover, specifically leather purpose-tanned for footballs. When peasants first covered pig bladders with leather, they did so with whatever leather was lying around. Likewise, cobblers covered footballs using the leather purchased for their primary business: shoemaking. They may have selected specific leather or portions of the hide better suited to making footballs than shoes, but they did not work at a scale that warranted developing leathers specially tanned for footballs.

The situation changed with the rise of sporting goods companies selling their wares through nationwide catalogs. Many of these firms emerged from the slaughterhouse and tanning businesses, so they understood differences in leather, allowing them to treat or tan leather to retain its pebbling and limit water absorption. Less water-absorbent balls did not gain weight as the game went on, retained their shape, and did not stiffen after drying out. Early manufacturers had limited success developing leather with the desired properties, but most still claimed they had the magic formula.

By the 1940s, however, innovation in football leathermaking shifted from ensuring durability to enhancing the ball's grip, seemingly in response to the challenge posed by rubber footballs. The emphasis on grip focused on quarterbacks and others who threw the ball forward. In addition to improving the leather to maintain its pebbling, other improvements, such as Horween Leather's Grip-Tite and Tanned-in-Tack, enhanced the ball's grip by making the leather tackier.

Improving the grip and durability of football leathers, enhanced linings, and the move to urethane bladders have all contributed to improved durability and quality control of footballs. The NFL and Wilson drove the post-WWII improvements, which are consistent with the NFL's push toward consistency and uniformity in many aspects of its operations.

**Changes in Appearance**

The original role of branding footballs involved burning trademarks and other information into the leather to indicate that football's governing organization sanctioned the ball. Designating an official brand and model allowed the governing body to eliminate arguments about which ball to use in games, much as following consistent rules eliminated the pre-game conflicts about game rules one decade earlier.

Shifting from an approved brand and model to a set of specifications opened the door to many sporting goods manufacturers supplying balls meeting those specifications. It inadvertently allowed manufacturers to produce bootleg balls that did not meet the requirements and balls with added but unregulated features such as colors and stripes. The coloring and striping of balls varied until the NFHS codified a design for the 1953 season, and we have largely seen only variation on that theme since then.

Gridiron footballs passed through the colored-ball phase and returned to the traditional tanned leather ball, a position that differs from the inflated balls used in other sports worldwide.

**Future Changes to the Football**

Football and sports generally are increasingly high-tech. Football players wear monitors to track the impacts registered on their helmets, heart rates, and movements on the field. Now, sensors are being added to footballs to allow the ball to be spotted correctly in line-to-gain and goal-line situations.

How the football will change in the future is unknowable, but history suggests that future changes will be due to larger forces affecting the game. Given the role of the media in funding the highest levels of football, future changes to the ball will likely benefit the viewing audience or real-time analysis of games.

Until then, the football's leather cover, which arrived well before the Industrial Revolution began, will remain our image of the football and keep us tied to the game's pig bladder-kicking origins.

At least, that's what I know about the football's evolution as of July 2024.

# NOTES

## 1. Shapes and Sizes

1. Stagg, A. A., and W.W. Stout. *Touchdown!* New York: Longmans, Green and Co., 1927.; Wilson, Jonathon. *Inverting The Pyramid: The History of Soccer Tactics.* Bold Type Books. 2008.
2. Collins, Tony. *How Football Began.* London: Routledge. 2019.
3. Hughes, Thomas. *Tom Brown's School Days.* McMillan: London, 1857.
4. Football, Rugby Football Union,' *Field (London),* September 17, 1892.
5. Wilson, Jonathon. *Inverting The Pyramid: The History of Soccer Tactics.* Bold Type Books. 2008.
6. Gilbert, James. *The Gilbert Story. Rugby Football.* Aldeburgh, UK: Robin Summers. 1957.
7. Chadwick, Henry (Ed.). *Beadle's Dime Book of Cricket and Foot-Ball,* New York: Beadle and Adams. 1866.
8. Bennett, Timothy, Assistant Director of Strategic Communications, Yale Athletics. Personal communication. June 4, 2024.
9. 'The Game Of Football,' *Indianapolis Journal,* October 16, 1887.
10. Davis, Parke H. *Football: The American Intercollegiate Game.* New York: Charles Scribner's Sons, 1911.
11. Camp, Walter (Ed.). *Spalding's 1890 Official Foot Ball Guide.* New York: American Sports Publishing. 1890.
12. 1896. 'New Football Rules,' *Boston Globe,* April 26, 1896.
13. 'The Game of Football,' *Indianapolis Journal,* October 16, 1887.
14. 'Yale Men Enraged,' *New York Times,* October 11, 1886.
15. Nelson, David M. *Anatomy of a Game: Football, the Rules, and the Men Who Played the Game.* University of Delaware Press. 1994
16. Storck, Carl L. (Ed) *Official Guide of the National Football League.* New York: American Sports Publishing. 1939.
17. Lio, Augie, 'Dawson Once Had Doubt About Grid Career; Now Set For Packers,' *Herald-News (Passaic, NJ),* January 13, 1967.

## 2. Bladders, Lacing, and Valves

1. Camp, Walter and Lorin F. Deland, 'Scientific Football,' Buffalo Courier Express, October 4, 1896.
2. 'Buttonhook Pierces Galeton Boy's Eyelid,' Star Gazette (Elmira, NY), December 4, 1915.
3. Camp, Walter, 'Has New Method of Inflating Ball,' Jersey Observer and Jersey Journal (Jersey City, NJ), March 21, 1923.
4. Hall, E. K. (Ed.) *National Collegiate Athletic Association Official Foot Ball Guide.* New York: American Sports Publishing. 1929.
5. 1928-1929 Wilson Catalog Fall and Winter

## 4. Materials and Manufacturing

1. Advertisement. *Foot-Ball Rules and Referee's Book*. Boston: American Intercollegiate Association. 1889.
2. 1927-28 GoldSmith Fall and Winter Catalog
3. Baldwin, Doug, 'Doug-Outs,' *Californian (Salinas)*, December 6, 1952.
4. Cooke, Jr., Homer F. (Ed.) *National Collegiate Athletic Association Official Football Guide*. New York: National Collegiate Athletic Bureau. 1952.
5. Cooke, Jr., Homer F. (Ed.) *National Collegiate Athletic Association Official Football Guide*. New York: National Collegiate Athletic Bureau. 1956.
6. Cooke, Jr., Homer F. (Ed.) *National Collegiate Athletic Association Official Football Guide*. New York: National Collegiate Athletic Bureau. 1957.
7. Gilbert, James. *The Gilbert Story*. Rugby Football. Aldeburgh, UK: Robin Summers. 1957.
8. 1928 D&M Catalog

## 5. Game and Practice Footballs

1. 'Princeton's Commencement,' *Baltimore Sun*, June 22, 1886. - cropped
2. 'The Princeton Boys,' Kansas City Journal, November 25, 1892
3. Camp, Walter. Spalding's 1918 Official Foot Ball Guide. New York: American Sports Publishing. 1918.
4. 'Rugby World Cup 2023 Match Balls Made Available to Fans Worldwide by Match-WornShirt,' *Licensing International*, September 28, 2023. Accessed April 12, 2024:
    https://licensinginternational.org/news/rugby-world-cup-2023-match-balls-made-available-to-fans-worldwide-by-matchwornshirt/

# BIBLIOGRAPHY

The Bibliography lists selected sources in order of their first use and generally excludes sources mentioned in the text.

## CHAPTER 1: SHAPE AND SIZE

### Football in the United Kingdom
Collins, Tony, host. 'Why Is The Rugby Ball Oval?' *Rugby Reloaded*. June 13, 2022. https://tony-collins.squarespace.com/rugbyreloaded/2022/6/9/rugby-reloaded-188-why-is-the-rugby-ball-oval

Collins, Tony. *How Football Began: A Global History of How the World's Football Codes Were Born*. London: Routledge. 2019.

Collins, Tony. *The Oval World: A Global History of Football*. London: Bloomsbury. 2015.

Richard Lindon & Co. Rugby England. Accessed January 22, 2019. http://richardlindon.co.uk

### England's Rugby Ball
Hughes, Thomas. *Tom Brown's Schooldays*. London: Macmillan. 1857

Gilbert, James. *The Gilbert Story. Rugby Football*. Aldeburgh, UK: Robin Summers. 1957.

### An Evolving Game
Collins, Tony, 'Unexceptional Exceptionalism: The Origins of American football in a Transnational Context,' *Journal of Global History*, July 2013.

Davis, Parke H. *Football: The American Intercollegiate Game*. New York: Charles Scribner's Sons, 1911.

### The American Ball and American Rugby Ball
'Yale Men Enraged,' *New York Times*, October 11, 1886.

'Foot-Ball,' *Outing*, December 1886.

Camp, Walter. *Spalding's 1890 Official Foot Ball Guide*. New York: American Sports Publishing. 1890.

Chadwick, Henry (Ed.). Beadle's Dime Book of Cricket and Foot-Ball, New York - Beadle and Adams. 1866.

*Rules*. Montreal: Foot Ball Association of Canada Rules, Rugby Union. 1873.

Brown, Timothy P. *How Football Became Football: 150 Years of the Game's Evolution*. West Bloomfield, MI: Brown House Publishing. 2020.

Personal communication. Timothy Bennett. Assistant Director of Strategic Communications, Yale University. June 4, 2024.

### Toward A Smaller Ball
'Editorial Notes,' *Buffalo Courier Express*, November 27, 1876.

'The Game of Football,' *Indianapolis Journal*, October 16, 1887.

Camp, Walter. Spalding's Official Foot Ball Guide. American Sports Publishing: New York. 1892.

# Bibliography

Camp, Walter. Spalding's Official Foot Ball Guide. American Sports Publishing: New York. 1896.
'The Football Season,' *Hartford Courant*, September 14, 1898.

**Spalding Model J to J5**
Camp, Walter. Spalding's Official Foot Ball Guide. American Sports Publishing: New York. 1899 through 1911.
'Many Important Points Football Rules Committee Should Decide,' *St. Louis Post-Dispatch*, December 27, 1909.

**When Football Came to Pass**
'Smaller Ball Will Give All Elevens Chance at Forward Pass,' *St. Louis Globe-Democrat*, December 6, 1906.

**The 1912 Specifications**
Camp, Walter. Spalding's 1912 Official Foot Ball Guide. American Sports Publishing: New York. 1912.

**Bootleg Balls and 1929 Rule Changes**
'Football Rules Committee Takes Steps To Abolish "Bootleg Ball,"' *Indianapolis Star*, March 6, 1929.
'New Football Rules, Bootleg Ball Evil Is Eliminated By New Code For 1929,' *Stockton Evening and Sunday Record*, October 23, 1929.
'Bootleg Ball Not Used By 1929 Teams,' *North Adams Transcript (MA)*, November 14, 1929.
Hall, E. K. (Ed). *Official Football Rules of the National Collegiate Athletic Association*. American Sports Publishing: New York. 1929

**1934 Size Reduction**
'Smaller Football Will Aid Passers, Test Drop Kickers,' *Decatur Herald*, March 31, 1934.
'Could Hold Nationals In Hawaii,' *Honolulu Star-Bulletin*, April 4, 1934.
'Billikens Given The New 1934 Stream-Lined Football A Test,' *St. Louis Star and Times*, August 2, 1934.
Templeton, Dink, 'Narrower Ball Cuts Down Number Of Fumbles: Templeton,' *San Francisco Examiner*, October 8, 1934.
'Colgate Coach Explains New Football Rules,' *Binghamton Press*, October 20, 1934.
Okeson, W. R. (Ed). *Official Football Rules of the National Collegiate Athletic Association*. American Sports Publishing: New York. 1934.

**The Ball Since 1934**
Frog, Avalanche Gridiron Coaches Get All 'Balled ' Up,' *Fort Worth Star-Telegram*, December 31, 1936.
'New Grid Rules Require Home Team To Provide Rigidly Tested Ball,' *Atlanta Journal*, January 8, 1939.

**NFL and AFL Balls**
*Official Football Rules of the National Football League*. American Sports Publishing: New York. 1939.
Oldham, Scott, Bombs Away, *Popular Mechanics*, October 2001.
'How Wilson And "The Duke" Became The Official NFL Football,' W Blog, Accessed April 1, 2024. https://www.wilson.com/en-us/blog/football/behind-scenes/how-wilson-and-

# Bibliography

%E2%80%9C-duke%E2%80%9D-became-official-nfl-football#
'Dr. Ryan All Balled-Up,' *Star-Gazette (Elmira, NY)*, January 14, 1967.
Scholl, Bill, 'They'll Have A Ball Today, But Which?, *Democrat and Chronicle (Rochester, NY)*, January 15, 1967.
Leifeste, Tim, "I And Other Small Sports,' *San Angelo Standard-Times*, September 11, 1969.

## The CFL Ball
'Some CFLers Don't Like Ball,' Leader-Post, June 19, 1985.
'A Tanderdemallion Kid And His Dog,' *Vancouver Sun*, December 1, 1990.
'Chronology of the CFL,' *Commercial Appeal (Memphis)*, November 17, 1994.
'Frequently Asked Questions About Equipment,' CFLdb, https://cfldb.ca/faq/equipment/. Accessed May 16, 2024.

## CHAPTER 2: BLADDERS, LACING, AND VALVES

### Inflating and Lacing Early Footballs
Harrington, James, 'Explained: Why a rugby ball is that shape?, Rugby World, February 6, 2024. Access May 1, 2024. https://www.rugbyworld.com/takingpart/rugby-basics/explained-rugby-ball-shape-158070

### Along Came Valves
'Heisman Springs New Valves for Footballs,' *Boston Globe*, March 10, 1923.
Camp, Walter, 'Has New Method Of Inflating Ball,' *Jersey Observer and Jersey Journal (Jersey City, NJ)*, March 21, 1923.
Davis, Ralph, 'A New Kind Of Football,' *Pittsburgh Press*, August 28, 1925.
'Irl Tubbs, University of Miami Football Coach, Is Inventor As Well As Gridiron Wizard, *Miami News*, July 10, 1935.
'Perfects New Inverted Valve,' *Battle Creek Enquirer*, May 5, 1925.

## CHAPTER 3: COLORS AND STRIPES

### Visibility
'Illinois Coach Protests Use Of Hidden Ball,' *Minneapolis Star*, October 26, 1926.
'Dispute Over Pads Worn By Penn Settled, *Rock Island Argus*, October 28, 1926.
'Friction In The Purple Eleven,' *Chicago Tribune*, October 24, 1901.
'Early Darkness Hurts Football,' *Philadelphia Inquirer*, October 29, 1918.

### Camouflage
'Grid Rules Body Moves To Curb "Sharp Practices",' *Albert Lea Tribune*, March 26, 1930.
'They'll Use Yellow Football in U.C. Game --- There's Good Reason,' *Cincinnati Post*, October 2, 1930.
'First Big Ten Game At Night,' *Chicago Tribune*, October 6, 1935.
'White Stripes on Brown Ball, Will Be Used in Game Tonight' *Greely Daily Tribune*, October 9, 1936.
Nelson, David M. *Anatomy of a Game: Football, the Rules, and the Men Who Played the Game*. University of Delaware Press. 1994.

### Striping
1949 MacGregor GoldSmith Fall and Winter catalog
'Modify Prep Grid Substitutions,' *Akron Beacon Journal*, January 6, 1952.

*Official Football Rules*. Chicago: National Federation of State High School Athletic Associations. 1953.
'Packers Eye Tackle, Big Back in Draft,' *Green Bay Press-Gazette*, January 17, 1956.
'NCAA Adopts 94 Rule Changes,' *News-Press (Fort Myers)*, January 17, 1974.

**Right and Left-Handed Footballs**
'Left-Handed Football,' *Oakland Tribune*, August 19, 1970.
Bretag, Gerry, 'Davenport Grid Club Hears Gamber, Coaches,' *Quad-City Times (Davenport, IA)*, September 22, 1970.
'Stabler and Left-Handed Pigskin,' *Sacramento Bee*, December 29, 1978.
Davis, Craig,' Quantum Leaps,' *South Florida Sun Sentinel (Fort Lauderdale)*, September 6, 1990.
'By Rule, Football Can't Change Its Stripes,' *Tampa Bay Times*, December 8, 1997.
Ross, Alan, 'The White, Night Football,' *Coffin Corner*, Vol. 21, No. 2, 1999.

**The Visually Enhanced Ball**
Slater, Jim, 'Finley Debuts Brighter Football,' *United Press International*, August 30, 1989.
Scorecard, *Sports Illustrated*, October 23, 1989.
'New Footballs Add Color To Sport,' *Indianapolis News*, November 2, 1989.
'Blue-Gray Tilt To Introduce New Football,' *Grand Island Independent (NE,)* November 24, 1989.
'Group Move To Save Star Track,' *News Tribune (Tacoma)*, January 18, 1990.

**Branding**
'Ask The Globe – Sports,' *Boston Globe*, March 3, 1985.
Pressgrove, Andy, 'Colleges Insist On Using Own Ball,' *Town Talk (Alexandria, LA)*, October 21, 1986.
Lowitt, Bruce, 'By Rule, Football Can't Change Its Stripes,' *Tampa Bay Times*, December 8, 1997.

**CHAPTER 4: MATERIALS AND MANUFACTURING**

**Pigskin, Sheepskin, Horsehide, and Cowhide**
'Polo,' *New York Daily Herald*, October 8, 1876.
'Footballs,' *Fall River Daily Evening News*, November 11, 1893.
'Camp Discusses Football Changes,' *Evening Journal (Wilmington, DE)*, September 4, 1912.
Green, Dudley, 'Vanderbilt Grid Squad To Practice In Short During Hot Morning Drills,' *Nashville Banner*, August 28, 1953.

**Rubber Footballs Bounce Back**
'Origin Of Footballs,' *Democrat and Chronicle (Rochester, NY)*, March 26, 1901.
'Early Football,' *Daily Republican (Phoenixville, PA)*, November 5, 1915.
Rice, Grantland, The Sportlight, *Dayton Daily News*, August 31, 1934.
Roberts, Don, 'Out Of Bounds,' *La Grande Observer*, April 17, 1948.
Taylor, 'Sec,' 'Sittin' In With The Athletes, *Des Moines Register*, June 15, 1950.
'The Term 'Pigskin' May Be Out With Advent Of Rubber Footballs, *Nashville Banner*, September 27, 1951.
'Something New In Footballs,' *Nashville Banner*, October 13, 1951.
'Rubber 'Pigskin' Satisfies,' *Newsday (Melville, NY)*, October 31, 1951.
Baldwin, Doug, 'Doug-Outs,' *Californian (Salinas)*, December 6, 1952.

## Bibliography

'The Voit Football Basketball News,' *Journal of the American Association for Health, Physical Education, Recreation,* January 1954.

Reinhardt, Randy, 'Moving Hash Marks To Help Offense,' *Pantagraph (Bloomington, IL),* August 26, 1993.

**Getting a Grip**

'Pebbled Leather: Pebbled To Perfection,' Carl Friedrik Magazine. Accessed May 1, 2024. https://www.carlfriedrik.com/magazine/what-is-pebbled-leather

The Fair advertisement. *Chicago Chronicle,* October 31, 1896.

Brown, Timothy P., *Today's Tidbit... The Horween Brothers and the NFL.* Football Archaeology. Accessed April 10, 2024. https://www.footballarchaeology.com/p/todays-tidbit-the-horween-brothers

'Notion Kicked Around For Years Is Thrown For Loss-Footballs Are Cowhide Not Pigskin,' *Chicago Tribune,* September 30, 1954.

'Hank Casserly Says,' *Capital Times (Madison, WI),* January 12, 1955.

Oldham, Scott, Bombs Away, *Popular Mechanics,* October 2001.

**Stickum**

All About Those Leather Suits,' *Boston Globe,* November 26, 1893.

'How Yale Team Upset Plans,' *Harrisburg Telegraph,* December 27, 1932.

Walton, Bob, 'BOB-ing Along,' *San Bernardino County Sun,* October 2, 1937.

Pompei, Dan, 'How the NFL Cheats,' *Bleacher Report,* September 9, 2016. Accessed January 2, 2016. https://bleacherreport.com/articles/2656747-how-the-nfl-cheats-foreign-substances

**The Grip Enhanced Football**

'Finley Gets Grip On Footballs,' *Indianapolis News,* September 6, 1990.

Kaneshiro, Stacy, 'Double Grip Ball To Make Debut,' *Honolulu Observer,* December 25 1990.

Bryant, Tim, 'Rawlings, Finley At Odds Over 'Dimpled' Football,' *St. Louis Post-Dispatch,* August 13, 1992.

'Perles Uses TV Show To Make Sales Pitch,' *Detroit Free Press,* November 22, 1992.

Sapardanis, Steve, 'The Reverse Dimple Rawlings Double Grip Football, Storytime with Sap,' mvictors.com, October 21, 2014. Accessed May 1, 2024. https://mvictors.com/the-reverse-dimple-rawlings-double-grip-football-storytime-with-sap/

**Two, Four, and Eight-Panel Balls**

McLemore, Henry, 'New 'Eight-Seam' Football To Start Revolt Among Coaches, Says Critic,' Los Angeles Evening Express, September 4, 1931.

Gould, Jay, 'Sports Slants, *Ithaca Journal,* September 16, 1931.

'New Grid Oval Lacks Bounce Of 4-Seamer,' *Brooklyn Daily-Eagle,* October 11, 1931.

'Here's New "Rabbit" Ball-It's Livelier,' *Wichita Beacon,* October 23, 1933.

'Here's New 'Rabbit' Ball – Men Who Kick It,' *Greenville News (SC),* October 28, 1933.

Okeson, W. R. (Ed). *Official Football Rules of the National Collegiate Athletic Association.* American Sports Publishing: New York. 1932

**Manufacturing Footballs**

'Making A Football,' *Ironwood News-Record (MI),* April 15, 1899.

'Footballs Are Not Made Of Pigskin, As Generally Believed, But Calfskin,' *Brooklyn Daily Eagle,* November 5, 1911.

'An Old Fallacy Is Corrected,' *Daily Gate City and Constitution Democrat (Keokuk, IA)*, November 2, 1917.
'Pigskins From Cowhide,' *Pittsburgh Press*, October 6, 1940.
McCarty, Bob. 'Here's The Pitch,' *Sacramento Union*, October 28, 1960.
Kahler, Kayln, 'From Farm to Field, and Every Point Between: How a Cow Becomes a Football,' *Sports Illustrated*, January 29, 2019.
'From Watermelon To Wilson: The 100-Year History Of The Football,' Popular Mechanics, January 26, 2023. Accessed May 1, 2024. https://www.popularmechanics.com/adventure/sports/a42678560/how-footballs-are-made/

## CHAPTER 5: GAME AND PRACTICE BALLS

**Game Balls**
'Princeton's Commencement,' *Baltimore Sun*, June 22, 1886.
'The Princeton Boys,' *Kansas City Journal*, November 25, 1892.
'Cutting Pigskin,' *Journal (Meriden, CT)*, November 11, 1899.
'Yale Pays Pretty Compliment to Dartmouth, Given Tie-Game Ball,' *Buffalo Courier*, October 21, 1924.
Benagh, Jim, 'A Visit With Fritz Crisler Is Like Reliving 'The Evolution of Football'', *Detroit Free Press*, August 1, 1976.
'Rugby World Cup 2023 Match Balls Made Available to Fans Worldwide by MatchWornShirt,' *Licensing International*, September 28, 2023. Accessed April 12, 2024: https://licensinginternational.org/news/rugby-world-cup-2023-match-balls-made-available-to-fans-worldwide-by-matchwornshirt/

**Tethered Football**
Dolan, Jr., William J. Patent #1655599, Official Gazette of the United States Patent Office, January 10, 1928. Filed June 21, 1923.

**Weighted Footballs**
Allen, George H. *Encyclopedia Of Football Drills*. New Jersey: Prentice-Hall, 1954.
Allen, George H. *Complete Book of Winning Football Drills*. Englewood Cliffs: Prentice Hall, 1960.
'Starr, Quiet Celebrity, Is A Nice Guy Finishing First,' *Kenosha News*, August 27, 1968.
Hess, Jr., Chuck, 'Chuck 'n Sports,' *Evening Independent (Massillon)*, August 16, 1971.

# ACKNOWLEDGMENTS

Writing a book's Acknowledgments is one of the pleasures of being an author. The act indicates the book is complete while allowing one to reflect on those who contributed to the finished product.

As in the past, a heartfelt thank you goes to the librarians, archivists, and reference personnel at universities and other institutions who have scanned historic images and volumes to make them available to the masses. Some individuals in the same group process requests to use those images in publications and they are always eager to help researchers in need. So, I give thanks to the world's librarians.

While not a librarian, I am grateful to Timothy Bennett of Yale University Athletics for taking the time to identify the keeper of a trophy case key so he could measure and confirm the size of the oldest known American rugby football.

I am also indebted to Tony Collins, the author of numerous books on the history of rugby and other football codes. He helped shape my thinking about how American football connected with the other football codes and directly contributed information and insights to this effort.

Other amateur historians or hobbyists contributed images from their collections. John Gennantonio, in particular, graciously provided several images seen here.

John Valentine and other Canadian Football Research Society members provided fact-finding assistance, though we have yet to find a definitive answer to my main question. That's just the way it works.

Others, especially Darin Hayes, whom I join on his weekly podcast, help keep the enthusiasm for football history flowing. Jeffrey Payne and others on the Vintage Football Community forum also responded to various queries and suggested potential sources.

Thanks to the *Football Archaeology* subscribers who had access to an near-finished, serialized version of *A History of the Football*. A couple offered corrections or their thoughts on its content or style.

Of course, my deepest thanks go to my family, who seem to support my digging new rabbit holes while documenting football's history. Their support is always appreciated.

# ALSO BY TIMOTHY P. BROWN

Fields of Friendly Strife: The Doughboys and Sailors of the WWI Rose Bowls
How Football Became Football: 150 Years of the Game's Evolution
Hut! Hut! Hike!: A History of Football Terminology

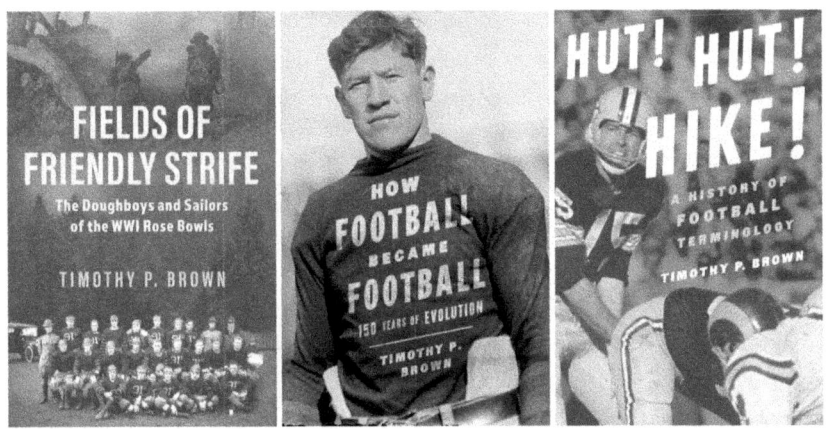

Other writings by Timothy P. Brown are available at:
Football Archaeology
https://www.footballarchaeology.com/

8/2024

www.ingramcontent.com/pod-product-compliance
Lightning Source LLC
Chambersburg PA
CBHW070547090426
42735CB00013B/3092